M000099163

RTI Applications, Volume 2

The Guilford Practical Intervention in the Schools Series

Kenneth W. Merrell, Founding Editor
T. Chris Riley-Tillman, Series Editor

www.guilford.com/practical

This series presents the most reader-friendly resources available in key areas of evidence-based practice in school settings. Practitioners will find trustworthy guides on effective behavioral, mental health, and academic interventions, and assessment and measurement approaches. Covering all aspects of planning, implementing, and evaluating high-quality services for students, books in the series are carefully crafted for everyday utility. Features include ready-to-use reproducibles, lay-flat binding to facilitate photocopying, appealing visual elements, and an oversized format. Recent titles have purchaser-only companion Web pages where the reproducible materials can be downloaded and printed.

RECENT VOLUMES

Response to Intervention, Second Edition: Principles and Strategies for Effective Practice
Rachel Brown-Chidsey and Mark W. Steege

Child and Adolescent Suicidal Behavior:
School-Based Prevention, Assessment, and Intervention
David N. Miller

Cognitive Therapy for Adolescents in School Settings
Torrey A. Creed, Jarrod Reisweber, and Aaron T. Beck

Motivational Interviewing for Effective Classroom Management: The Classroom Check-Up
Wendy M. Reinke, Keith C. Herman, and Randy Sprick

Positive Behavior Support in Secondary Schools: A Practical Guide
Ellie L. Young, Paul Caldarella, Michael J. Richardson, and K. Richard Young

Academic and Behavior Supports for At-Risk Students: Tier 2 Interventions
Melissa Stormont, Wendy M. Reinke, Keith C. Herman, and Erica S. Lembke

RTI Applications, Volume 1: Academic and Behavioral Interventions
Matthew K. Burns, T. Chris Riley-Tillman, and Amanda M. VanDerHeyden

Coaching Students with Executive Skills Deficits
Peg Dawson and Richard Guare

Enhancing Instructional Problem Solving:
An Efficient System for Assisting Struggling Learners
John C. Begeny, Ann C. Schulte, and Kent Johnson

Clinical Interviews for Children and Adolescents, Second Edition: Assessment to Intervention
Stephanie H. McConaughy

RTI Team Building: Effective Collaboration and Data-Based Decision Making
Kelly Broxterman and Angela J. Whalen

RTI Applications, Volume 2: Assessment, Analysis, and Decision Making
T. Chris Riley-Tillman, Matthew K. Burns, and Kimberly Gibbons

Daily Behavior Report Cards: An Evidence-Based System of Assessment and Intervention
Robert J. Volpe and Gregory A. Fabiano

RTI Applications, Volume 2

Assessment, Analysis, and Decision Making

T. Chris Riley-Tillman
Matthew K. Burns
Kimberly Gibbons

THE GUILFORD PRESS
New York   London

© 2013 The Guilford Press
A Division of Guilford Publications, Inc.
72 Spring Street, New York, NY 10012
www.guilford.com

All rights reserved

Except as indicated, no part of this book may be reproduced, translated, stored in a retrieval
system, or transmitted, in any form or by any means, electronic, mechanical, photocopying,
microfilming, recording, or otherwise, without written permission from the publisher.

Printed in the United States of America

This book is printed on acid-free paper.

Last digit is print number: 9 8 7 6 5 4 3 2 1

LIMITED PHOTOCOPY LICENSE

These materials are intended for use only by qualified professionals.

The publisher grants to individual purchasers of this book nonassignable permission to
reproduce all materials for which photocopying permission is specifically granted in a
footnote. This license is limited to you, the individual purchaser, only for personal use or use
with individual clients or students. This license does not grant the right to reproduce these
materials for resale, redistribution, electronic display, or any other purposes (including but not
limited to books, pamphlets, articles, video- or audiotapes, blogs, file-sharing sites, Internet or
intranet sites, and handouts or slides for lectures, workshops, or webinars, whether or not a fee
is charged). Permission to reproduce these materials for these and any other purposes must be
obtained in writing from the Permissions Department of Guilford Publications.

The authors have checked with sources believed to be reliable in their efforts to provide
information that is complete and generally in accord with the standards of practice that are
accepted at the time of publication. However, in view of the possibility of human error or changes
in behavioral, mental health, or medical sciences, neither the authors, nor the editors and publisher,
nor any other party who has been involved in the preparation or publication of this work warrants
that the information contained herein is in every respect accurate or complete, and they are not
responsible for any errors or omissions or the results obtained from the use of such information.
Readers are encouraged to confirm the information contained in this book with other sources.

Library of Congress Cataloging-in-Publication Data

Riley-Tillman, T. Chris.
    RTI applications / T. Chris Riley-Tillman, Matthew K. Burns, Kimberly Gibbons.
        p. cm. — (The Guilford practical intervention in the schools series)
    Includes bibliographical references and index.
    Contents: v. 2. Academic and behavioral interventions
    ISBN 978-1-4625-0914-0 (pbk.)
    1. Response to intervention (Learning disabled children)—Handbooks, manuals, etc. I. Burns,
Matthew K. II. Gibbons, Kimberly. III. Title.
    LC4705.B87 2012
    371.9—dc23
                                                                    2011044444

*In memory of Ken Merrell,
whose vision for The Guilford Practical Intervention in the Schools Series
framed this book, and whose leadership in school psychology
helped shape the profession*

About the Authors

T. Chris Riley-Tillman, PhD, is Associate Professor in the Department of Educational, School, and Counseling Psychology at the University of Missouri. His research focuses on improving education through the effective application of a problem-solving model. Specifically, he is interested in social behavioral assessment, intervention, single-case design, and consultation. Dr. Riley-Tillman has published numerous articles, books, and book chapters related to these research interests. He is the Series Editor of The Guilford Practical Intervention in the Schools Series.

Matthew K. Burns, PhD, is Professor of Educational Psychology, Coordinator of the School Psychology Program, and Co-Director of the Minnesota Center for Reading Research at the University of Minnesota. He is the Editor of *School Psychology Review* and a former Editor of *Assessment for Effective Intervention*. Dr. Burns has conducted research on response to intervention (RTI), assessment of instructional levels, academic interventions, and facilitating problem-solving teams. He has published numerous articles and book chapters and has coauthored and coedited several books.

Kimberly Gibbons, PhD, is Executive Director of the St. Croix River Education District in Rush City, Minnesota. She was named "Outstanding Administrator of the Year" by the Minnesota Administrators of Special Education (MASE) and was recently elected President of the MASE. Dr. Gibbons has been responsible for supporting implementation of RTI frameworks in her school districts for the past 17 years, and was instrumental in changing state education laws to include RTI language. She provides national consultation and has numerous publications, including several books, on RTI and data-based decision making.

Acknowledgments

We begin by thanking our many mentors who have helped shape our beliefs and practices over the years. We also thank Natalie Graham, our editor at The Guilford Press, for her guidance. Finally, we express our gratitude to our families for their continued support.

Contents

536

UNIT 3

NO

CHAPTER 1

Advanced
Response-to-Intervention Applications

BEYOND THE "INTERVENTIONS"
IN RESPONSE TO INTERVENTION

Much has been written about response to intervention (RTI) over the last decade. Since its initial inclusion in the Individuals with Disabilities Education Improvement Act of 2004 (IDEIA), the model has been gaining momentum across the nation as the preferred method of service delivery for children. There is little need in this volume to review the history, varied definitions, or the future of RTI. That was accomplished in *RTI Applications, Volume 1: Academic and Behavioral Interventions*, as well as in a variety of articles, books, and websites (e.g., the National Center on Response to Intervention [*http://www.rti4success.org*] and the RTI Action Network [*www.rtinetwork.org*]). However, it is important to review the essential components of RTI that we believe drive the model.

1. RTI depends on a multi-tiered approach to intervention delivery with sufficient focus on the whole-school, small-group, and individual levels.
2. RTI is defined as a framework for using academic and behavior data to allocate resources to assist the greatest number of students in the most efficient way (Burns & Gibbons, 2012).
3. RTI requires an organizational structure that allows collaborative teams to review outcome data and make intervention decisions.

RTI is a schoolwide problem-solving model that, when implemented correctly, has the potential to provide the most effective instruction and intervention to each student. RTI is based on a three-tiered model (Tier 1: universal, Tier 2: targeted, and Tier 3: intensive), where increasing levels of intervention are provided to each student as he or she moves from Tier 1 to Tier 2 to Tier 3. The goal of RTI is to educate students in the least intensive

1

tier possible. Using this process, students with the most significant needs are identified for special education funding based on their response or lack of response to evidence-based intervention (EBI). While there are many other key issues when discussing RTI, these three key components provide the basis of the service delivery model. RTI is the systematic use of intervention across the tiers in an attempt to find the ideal manner in which to support students. Intervention decisions are guided by data, as are subsequent decisions about how best to serve a child (e.g., in Tier 1, 2, 3, or with/without a special education label).

Of course, it is not surprising that most of the attention goes to the word *intervention*, rather than the word *response*. As schools approach the significant task of mounting an RTI model, it makes a great deal of sense to focus primarily on intervention training and delivery. As reviewed in the first volume of *RTI Applications*, the "intervention" in RTI is not a simple concept, but rather a dramatic alteration of previous service delivery models. In an RTI model, school professionals not only need to be proficient in selecting both behavioral and academic EBIs, but also must be proficient at using interventions in a multi-tiered service delivery system. Specifically, EBI must be developed for Tier 1 (e.g., core curriculum), Tier 2 (e.g., small-group intervention practices), and Tier 3 (e.g., functionally relevant individual interventions). Considering the complex differences among interventions across the tiers, this is a rather challenging task.

The process of selecting a schoolwide evidence-based curriculum can seem very different from testing a series of individual interventions for a child with significant behavior concerns. As such, much training and attention is necessary to build a school's skill base in the selection and implementation of a wide variety of approaches. Fundamentally, Volume 1 focused on that very topic, and should be considered as a resource for educational professionals to consider how to address this first step. Unfortunately, while effective selection of EBI is a necessary component of an RTI model, it is not sufficient. While intervention is obviously the heart of RTI, a comprehensive model of RTI involves far more than just successful intervention services.

Working from the base of multi-tiered EBIs there is a logical series of next steps. To measure the effectiveness of the EBI, it is critical that defensible formative assessment methods are selected, methods of evaluating the data are utilized, and decisions are made in a consistent manner. Each of these issues is addressed next, and represents the focus of this book.

THE ROLE OF OUTCOME DATA IN RESPONSE TO INTERVENTION

When one fully understands exactly what EBIs are, the necessity of data is obvious. EBIs are treatments that have been proven effective (to some degree) through outcome evaluations. As such, EBIs are likely to help change target behavior if implemented with integrity. While this definition of EBI does not suggest significant complexity, when one looks at the "fine print," issues arise.

The First "Fine-Print" Point of Evidence-Based Intervention

EBIs are validated for a particular purpose with a certain population. As such, specific EBIs are only useful for a particular range of problems (e.g., attention-
seeking children or accuracy-based reading difficulty)
and as such must be paired correctly with each case.

> **If you mismatch an EBI with a problem is it not designed to address, there is no reason to think that it will work.**

If you mismatch an EBI with a problem is it not designed to address, there is no reason to
think that it will work. A hammer is an effective tool, but not with a screw. In addition, one
should not assume that such a mismatch would be benign. Using an intervention designed
to work for a child who is misbehaving to receive attention when a child is actually misbehaving to escape adult attention can result in disaster. Going back to the hammer metaphor,
it is likely that a true strike of the hammer will damage the screw and possibly the hand
holding the screw.

The Second "Fine-Print" Point of Evidence-Based Intervention

EBI assumes that the treatment is used in the manner that it was researched. As such,
changing parts of an intervention, while typical, can invalidate the EBI. Unfortunately, it
is understood that in most cases EBIs are actually not implemented exactly as developed
(Sanetti, Gritter, & Dobey, 2011; Sanetti & Kratochwill, 2009). To be fair, a critical aspect
of teaching is indeed to customize the intervention to fit the case at hand. There are many
ways to change an intervention (frequency, materials, target, etc.) that can alter the effectiveness of the EBI, and EBI overviews rarely specify which steps can be altered and which
are actually critical aspects of the method. Thus we can expect that some well-selected
interventions will be altered in a manner that renders them ineffective.

The Third "Fine-Print" Point of Evidence-Based Intervention

EBIs are typically validated with large-group research or a series of small-group studies.
While large-group research is ideally suited for the documentation of the evidence base
for EBI there are implications to this approach. Specifically, it is common that within large
groups where EBIs have been documented as successful that there are cases where the
intervention was not effective. It is understood that a "strong" effect demonstrated across
10,000 children was not universally "strong" for all 10,000 children. In all likelihood, the
intervention was in fact ineffective for some children, but there were other cases where
there was a very strong impact that balanced out the cases with a weak or no effect. In the
end, validation that an intervention is "evidence-based" only means that the intervention is
more likely to be effective, not that it will be effective with all children. For an individual
case, the true documentation of "evidence based" is produced only after the intervention is
implemented and outcome data are produced that document a desired change in the target
behavior.

This fine print all leads to the conclusion that, while it is critical that educational professionals take care to select an appropriate EBI for each case and implement the intervention in a manner that does not to sap its effectiveness, one can never know whether it will indeed work until the outcome data document the child's response. Of course, this last sentence documents the critical need for formative data in an RTI model.

Discussing the need for data in an RTI model is, of course, nothing revolutionary. That being said, the authors of this book have an extensive history either consulting with or working in schools, and one of the common concerns is indeed the lack of a variety of assessment methods to produce the necessary outcome data. While there are numerous options when the referral concern is focused on reading fluency, the options dwindle when considering other academic issues (e.g., reading comprehension, math, writing, content areas) and behavior problems. In addition, there has been less development in creating assessment methods that focus on documenting integrity at the whole-school, small-group, and individual levels. To this end, in Chapters 2 and 3 we discuss how to approach the task of collecting data to support RTI models.

EVALUATING INTERVENTION

While intervention and assessment have received a great deal of attention in RTI literature, how the data are used is less frequently discussed. While it would seem simple to take the next step and do something with the data, the process is rather complicated. Several questions must be raised to consider what type of analyses are necessary, and whether specific experimental design is critical to defensible decision making.

1. Are the data related to a schoolwide, small-group, or individual child cases?
2. Is it critical to know whether the intervention (and only the intervention) has resulted in a change in the outcome data?
3. Is it acceptable to simply document that the child is getting better?

The answers to these questions can result in very different levels of required experimental control. For example, if it is acceptable to simply know whether a class or a child is "getting better" after an intervention has been implemented, then this process will be as simple as collecting baseline and intervention data and then examining the level gain, the trend of the data, or other relevant analysis approaches. On the other hand, if a case necessitates a team to specifically identify whether the child responded to an intervention, then it will require a more sophisticated approach to both how the intervention is implemented and the analysis methods utilized. The general category of approaches that outline the pathway to achieve the above goals in a defensible manner is single-case design (SCD) and analysis.

While rarely discussed in schools, SCD and analysis is a class of experimental methodology and related analytic approaches with a vibrant history in research and applied settings (Kazdin, 2011). SCD has been particularly useful for fields working with low-incidence populations. There are a number of terms used to describe SCD, including *single-subject*, *intrasubject,* and $N = 1$. We use the term *single-case,* as this approach can focus on a single subject or the comparison of groups (e.g., classrooms or schools). For the purpose of this book, the way we chose to introduce SCD was to consider what this class of methods has been designed to demonstrate. Specifically, SCDs have been developed to provide evidence to answer three questions (Cooper, Heron, & Heward, 2007; Johnston & Pennypacker, 1980; Riley-Tillman & Burns, 2009; Riley-Tillman & Wallcott, 2007):

1. Is there is a change in some dependent variable?
2. Is an observed change in the outcome data after an independent variable is presented specifically related to that independent variable?
3. Is this change generalizable to some other setting, target, or over time?

Although those goals of SCD may not immediately seem as relevant to modern education, when converted to focus on educational intervention specifically, the three general purposes of SCD become obvious:

1. Did the child's (or group's) behavior (e.g., percentage of time on task or mathematics fluency score) change after an EBI was implemented?
2. Was the observed change specifically related to the EBI?
3. Can the results of this intervention case be generalized to other similar educational problems and settings?

Each of these questions represents significant steps up in the experimental requirements that will require more focus later in the book. At this point, though, suffice it to say that the overall package allows educational professionals to defensibly document the effect of interventions, the specific role of the intervention in observed change, and whether that information has a more general programming utility.

It is fair for educational professionals to ask why we can't simply do interventions and see whether they work. In many cases this approach is indeed quite valid. For example, when using a whole-school reading curriculum, it is not important to truly know whether a child is learning to read due to that curriculum or whether some outside variable (e.g., tutoring, family reading support) is primarily responsible. In the end, when children respond to Tier 1 interventions we simply keep them in that system. This is a low-stakes decision, and not one that requires a high degree of conviction. On the other hand, in the case of a child who is being considered for a learning disability label in an RTI system due to the child's response to an intensive intervention that requires significant school resources, the necessity for schools to understand more thoroughly a child's response to intervention increases. Otherwise, the child could be labeled with an educational disability, a very high-stakes decision, without sufficient evidence that he or she actually is responding to the "necessary" intervention. Simply put, as the stakes rise in an RTI model, the necessity of both higher-quality data and high levels of experimental control increase (Riley-Tillman & Burns, 2009).

Chapter 4 explores the role of SCD in RTI and presents the necessary information for educational professionals to begin using it. Chapter 5 extends this discussion to issues of analysis of data in SCD. In this chapter, specific guidelines for how an educational professional should determine whether there is a change after the intervention is implemented is reviewed in depth.

DECISION MAKING IN RESPONSE TO INTERVENTION

Going back to one of the core concepts for RTI, the overarching goal is to find the ideal manner in which to provide intervention services to children based on their documented response to intervention at a variety of levels. For this to be possible, we not only need interventions, data, and experimental methods, but we also need a defensible set of methods to then make programmatic decisions about how best to work with a child. It is overly simplistic to say we simply need to document a child's response to invention and voila, we know what to do next. There are issues of multi-tiered intervention management and eligibility that require an organized decision-making process that is also evidence based. The multi-tiered nature of RTI results in different types of decisions throughout the model that require different approaches and level of rigor. For example, decisions at the group level will be made more quickly than eligibility decisions, but are no less essential to the overall effectiveness of RTI. In Chapters 6, 7, and 8 we examine decisions at the group and individual levels, as well as directly focus on eligibility decisions made within an RTI model.

> The overarching goal of RTI is to find the ideal manner in which to provide intervention services to children based on their documented response to intervention at a variety of levels.

RESPONSE TO INTERVENTION AND MULTI-TIERED SYSTEMS OF SUPPORT

Although RTI is the most common term used to discuss this class of schoolwide problem-solving models, there has been some push to use the broader term *multi-tiered system of support* (MTSS). The primary difference between traditional RTI and MTSS is the inclusion of a continuum of behavior interventions. A good way to think about the MTSS approach is presented by the Southern Maine Area Resource Team for Schools (*usm.main.edu/smart*). In this model, RTI–Academic (RTI-A or MTSS-A) is focused on academic interventions while RTI–Behavior (RTI-B or MTSS-B) is focused on behavior interventions. This model is highly consistent with both this book and Volume 1, which presented both academic and behavior interventions across a three-tiered approach. The final aspect of MTSS is RTI–Collaboration (RTI-C or MTSS-C), which focuses on educational professionals working together to understand and implement their role in the MTSS system. We have decided to use the term *RTI* throughout this book as it is the most often used at present, but we fully support the move to a comprehensive three-tiered model with both academic and behavior supports.

THE BOOK

In this book, we extend the focus of RTI to show teachers, administrators, school psychologists, and other educational professionals how to select assessment measures, evaluate the effectiveness of interventions, and make relevant decisions in an RTI model. As noted above, this book is intended to be used in conjunction with Volume 1, and typically by individuals who have at least a basic understanding of RTI. For readers with no experience with RTI, we suggest two books that provided a foundation for RTI use: *Implementing Response-to-Intervention in Elementary and Secondary Schools, Second Edition* by Burns and Gibbons (2012), and *Response to Intervention, Second Edition: Principles and Strategies for Effective Practice* by Brown-Chidsey and Steege (2010). The primary purpose of this book in particular, and both volumes of *RTI Applications* in general, is to provide guidance on some of the more complicated elements of RTI. As educational professionals who use RTI know, RTI practice can be very complex and technical. We believe that educational professions must have a detailed understanding for RTI to fulfill its vast potential for helping children.

This book focuses on the *R* in RTI. Once intervention is in place, it is critical to use assessment, design, and analysis to make defensible decisions about a child's response. These decisions guide educational professionals to provide children with the services they need. As noted above, this book is the second in a two-volume set. In the first book we addressed intervention. It is important to note that the current book has been designed to accompany a multi-tiered, and multifaceted (academic and behavioral) approach to intervention. This book moves from that base of effective intervention design and implementation to provide the tools for school-based practitioners to develop a comprehensive RTI service delivery model. Specifically, Chapters 2 and 3 address assessment in a multi-tiered service delivery model (Chapter 2) and formative academic and behavioral assessment (Chapter 3). Then Chapters 4 and 5 move to an overview of the role of single-case design (Chapter 4) and data analysis (Chapter 5) in a defensible RTI service delivery model. Finally, Chapters 6–8 focus on decisions about groups (Chapter 6), decisions about individual students (Chapter 7), and special education decision making (Chapter 8). We conclude with a discussion of building-level RTI professional development in Chapter 9.

> Once intervention is in place, it is critical to use assessment, design, and analysis to make defensible decisions about a child's response.

CHAPTER 2

School-Based Assessment

There are several key elements to RTI, but effective assessment is at the very core of any successful implementation model. In fact, we endorse a previous definition of RTI (Burns & VanDerHeyden, 2006) that conceptualized RTI as the systematic use of assessment data to most efficiently allocate resources in order to enhance learning for all students. Thus the primary purpose of assessment within an RTI model is to facilitate instructionally relevant data-based decision making. Data within an RTI model are used to identify the need for an intervention, identify which intervention is mostly likely to lead to success, determine whether an intervention resulted in adequate response, and in some cases, decide whether special education services are warranted (Ysseldyke, Burns, Scholin, & Parker, 2010). In this chapter we discuss assessment in general and the types of assessments that can most adequately inform an RTI model.

> The primary purpose of assessment within an RTI model is to facilitate instructionally relevant data-based decision making.

ASSESSMENT

The term *assessment* is used every day by practitioners from various fields and with varying connotations. We endorse the definition by the American Educational Research Association, American Psychological Association, and National Council for Measurement in Education (1999) that describes assessment as a decision-making process. Many terms that are used synonymously with assessment (e.g., testing) are actually potential components of an assessment process and do not have the same meaning. Specifically, assessment is an ongoing process of gathering information about student progress. Tests are one method to gather relevant data. Assessment processes lead to decisions that may or may not be valid, and the validity of the decisions must be evaluated within the purpose for which the data were gathered. There are no bad tests, just inappropriate uses of the data. Validity refers to the degree to which an assessment measures what it claims to measure, and no assessment tool or procedure is valid "for all purposes or in the abstract" (Sattler, 2001, p. 115). We do not discuss basic psychometric issues of reliability and validity, but instead apply the concepts to an RTI model.

Burns, Jacob, and Wagner (2008) reviewed research and assessment standards to conclude that an RTI process can lead to decisions that are fair, valid, comprehensive, multifaceted, and useful if the protocols within the model are carefully crafted, and interventions are based on a scientific problem-solving process that involves identifying and clarifying the problem, generating solutions, and measuring outcomes. Moreover, RTI models should rely on assessments for which research has consistently demonstrated instructional utility. Most assessment tools used in schools today are inconsistent with the assessment purposes within an RTI framework. For example, end-of-the-year tests are typically not useful for making intervention decisions. Moreover, problem analysis and school-based assessments have focused primarily on collecting historical data to identify internal and unalterable student characteristics. If the goal is to change student behavior or trajectory of learning, then estimates of previous behavior serve little purpose except to establish a baseline. However, when previous measures of student behavior are used to identify the environmental conditions that created or maintained the problem behavior in order to generate testable hypotheses, and those hypotheses are tested with ongoing data collection, then positive outcomes are more likely to occur. In other words, assessments within an RTI framework fit within Stiggins's (2005) model of assessment *for* learning rather than assessment *of* learning.

FORMATIVE EVALUATION

There are several ways to categorize various uses and formats of assessment, but we focus on the formative–summative continuum because this is the most central issue to an RTI framework. Bloom, Hastings, and Madaus (1971) delineated two purposes of assessment: formative evaluation: (1) "systematic evaluation in the process of curriculum construction, teaching, and learning for the purposes of improving any of these three processes," and (2) summative evaluation—the collection of data after instruction occurred to make judgments about the instruction such as "grading, certification, evaluation of progress, or research on effectiveness" (p. 117). The primary goal of summative evaluation is to determine how much has been learned or how much is being learned, but formative evaluation suggests specific objectives and items that need to be taught and how best to teach them (Stiggins, 2005).

Formative evaluation procedures are critical for improving student outcomes and are essential to effective RTI practice, and are probably best accomplished with samples of student behavior before, during, and after interventions occur. Monitoring student progress, usually with curriculum-based measurement (CBM), has become synonymous with formative evaluation (Deno, 2003; Silberglitt & Hintze, 2005), but those data are collected during or after interventions to determine their effectiveness, which is the very definition of summative evaluation (Bloom et al., 1971). Monitoring progress is an important aspect of an RTI framework, but if practitioners are interested in implementing a formative evaluation framework, which is needed for successful RTI implementation, then monitoring student progress is only scratching the surface.

Meta-analytic research found that most data collected before interventions, including IQ tests and standardized measures of reading, correlate quite well with pre- and post-intervention reading scores, but have minimal correlation with actual growth during the intervention (Burns & Scholin, in press). In other words, most standardized measures of IQ and reading predict who is a good reader and who needs help, but they do not predict for whom an intervention will be successful. Moreover, several researchers have suggested that practitioners should use data obtained from measures of various cognitive processes in order to determine appropriate reading interventions (Feifer, 2008; Fiorello, Hale, & Snyder, 2006; Hale, Fiorello, Bertin, & Sherman, 2003; Hale, Fiorello, Kavanagh, Hoeppner, & Gaither, 2001), but meta-analytic research found very small effects ($d \approx 0.20$) for interventions derived from measures of auditory or visual association, reception, and sequential memory (Kavale & Forness, 1999), and a recent meta-analysis found negligible effects for interventions derived from cognitive processing data ($g = 0.09$ to 0.17; Burns, Kanive, & Degrande,, 2012). Thus practitioners who use measures of cognitive processing as part of the intervention process are likely engaging in an ineffective practice based more on a resilient belief system than on research.

Although measures of cognitive processing do not suggest effective interventions because they lead to small effects, formative evaluation led to an average effect size of 0.71 (Fuchs & Fuchs, 1986), which suggested an effective practice. Why is formative evaluation so effective? Formative evaluation is characterized by data collected before instruction occurs (Linn & Gronlund, 2000), that are used to identify student needs and to plan instruction to better meet those needs (William, 2006). Thus formative evaluation should identify what to teach and how to teach it, which is probably best accomplished by direct samples of student behavior. This process results in the 0.71 effect size, suggesting effective practice. Below we discuss the characteristics of data that can be used to inform intervention and how those formative data fit within the purposes of an RTI model.

ASSESSMENT DATA
FOR RESPONSE-TO-INTERVENTION DECISIONS

Ysseldyke and colleagues (2010) suggested that in order for data to be considered within an intervention process, they should be evaluated for their precision, potential frequency of use, and sensitivity to change. However, these are not absolute terms because different levels of precisions, frequency, and sensitivity are needed depending on how the data are used. Remember, there is no such thing as a bad test or assessment—there are only misappropriate uses of the data. For example, if a measure was designed to screen students (i.e., identify students who need additional support), then the data would likely not be useful for designing interventions. Alternatively, some data are well designed to identify specific areas of student need, but do not offer reliable or global enough data to provide a screening of overall skill. Thus assessment tools must be evaluated within the context of how they are used.

Chapter 3 talks more specifically about uses of data to analyze problems, but here we discuss data that are used to (1) identify the need for an intervention, (2) identify which intervention is mostly likely to lead to success, (3) determine whether an intervention resulted in adequate response, and (4) decide whether special education services are warranted.

Identify Need for Intervention

The first decision within an RTI process is to determine who needs intervention through universal screening. Screening involves assessing all students with a measure of interest to determine whether additional support is needed to reach proficiency in that skill. There is considerable attention within the RTI research literature paid to screening students, which suggests that the measures used to do so should assess behaviors closely related to academic problems, should predict future academic outcomes (Jenkins, Hudson, & Johnson, 2007), and should align with the school's curriculum and instruction (Ikeda, Neessen, & Witt, 2008). Moreover, measures used to identify students who need additional support require a moderate level of psychometric adequacy, but there is room for some limited amount of error (Salvia, Ysseldyke, & Bolt, 2013).

> **The first decision within an RTI process is to determine who needs intervention through universal screening.**

The National Center on Response to Intervention rated various tools used to identify who needs additional support for academic problems and provides their ratings at *www.rti4success.org/screeningTools*. The criteria with which each tool is rated include evidence for reliability and validity, adequate norms, and the diagnostic accuracy of the tool. The measures listed in Table 2.1 were rated as demonstrating convincing evidence in all areas. There currently is not widely available rating of behavioral screening tools, but the recently funded National Center for Intensive Interventions (*www.intensiveintervention.org*) will soon provide a vetted rating of behavior measures that have potential as screening tools.

Precision

Data used for screening purposes should give global estimates of the skill. In other words, screening tools should assess reading, math, writing, overall adaptive behavioral functioning, and so forth. This concept is called a general outcome measure (GOM). GOMs are tools that can allow for statements about global estimates of key skills. The classic educational example of a GOM is CBM of reading that provides an efficient method to estimate a child's oral reading fluency (ORF). ORF provides a reliable and valuable estimate of reading, which is foundation skill critical to school success. Many assessment tools give estimates of specific skills (e.g., decoding skills, single-digit multiplication, time on task), but relying on those specific skill measures might result in misidentifying too many students because they may

TABLE 2.1. Assessment Tools Rated by the National Center on Response to Intervention as Demonstrating Convincing Evidence for All Areas

	Screening	Monitoring progress—general outcome	Monitoring progress—skill
Reading	• Edcheckup Oral Reading Fluency • Predictive Assessment of Reading • Star Reading	• Aimsweb Oral Reading Fluency • Aimsweb Letter-Naming Fluency • Aimsweb Letter-Sound Fluency • Aimsweb Nonsense Word Fluency • Aimsweb Phoneme Segmentation Fluency • Star Early Literacy • Star Reading	
Math	• Star Math	• Star Math	• Accelerated Math • Math Facts in a Flash

be strong in that one aspect of learning or behavior measured by the tool, but may lack skill in other important areas.

Frequency

Annual assessments do not provide information that is relevant to intervention efforts primarily because of the infrequency with which those data are collected (Shepard, 2000). However, screening data are only used for low-level decisions (e.g., who needs additional assistance), and for this task periodic assessment data may be quite helpful. Thus RTI models should contain periodic assessments, often referred to as benchmark assessments or interim assessments, in which general outcome data are collected for every child three to five times each year.

Sensitivity to Change

The primary purpose of screening measures is to identify students who need additional support. However, school personnel can use screening data to measure overall program effectiveness and to estimate student growth within one school year. Thus there needs to be some sensitivity to change, but the measures occur as infrequently as once every 16 weeks. As a result, the measures used to identify students do not need to be overly sensitive to change. More important, the screening measures need to adequately differentiate among students. Sensitivity within a screening framework is estimated by how well the data differentiate who will perform adequately on some future gold-standard criterion. More specifically, sensitivity is the how accurately a screening tool identifies students who will not perform well on a criterion measure, which for academic problems is frequently the state accountability test.

Identify Interventions

After students are identified as needing additional support, data are needed to help determine what intervention would most likely benefit each student because interventions that are closely matched to student skill result in improved learning and behavioral outcomes (Burns, 2007; Daly, Martens, Kilmer & Massie, 1996; Shapiro & Ager, 1992; Treptow, Burns, & McComas, 2007) and can have differential effects for individual students. As stated above, measures of cognitive processing, commonly referred to as an aptitude by treatment interaction, do not adequately inform the intervention selection process. However, a "skill by treatment interaction" (Burns, Codding, Boice, & Lukito, 2010), in which specific skills are measured to determine appropriate interventions, results in larger student effects. This is discussed more thoroughly in Chapter 3, and was extensively covered in Volume 1. Here we only discuss the type of measures that are appropriate for this process. Because these data are used for generating hypotheses, they would need to meet only a moderate level of psychometric adequacy. The data should probably be more reliable than those derived from screening measures (~0.70; Salvia et al., 2013), but a lower standard for diagnostic accuracy would be required. This lower level of reliability is acceptable, as any decisions will be subsequently tested.

Precision

Precision is a key component of measures used to identify interventions. It does not matter how well a child reads, for example; it matters how well he or she decodes r-controlled vowels, diagraphs, or diphthongs. In other words, reading fluency data are commonly collected in schools and can provide information about whether a child is struggling with reading fluency, but those data to not describe which specific skill deficits contribute to poor reading fluency or how to guide intervention. Thus intervention design decisions are heavily influenced by subskill mastery measures (SMMs), which assesses small domains of learning based on predetermined criteria for mastery (Fuchs & Deno, 1991). If a child struggles with reading, assessments of phonemic awareness and phonetic skills should be conducted to determine the appropriate intervention (Burns & Gibbons, 2012). Specific measures needed for mathematics skills could include knowledge of numeracy, basic fact fluency, and sign-to-operation correspondence (Fuchs et al., 2003). RTI has led to a resurgence in SMM with positive outcomes (Hosp & Ardoin, 2008; Ketterlin-Geller & Yovanoff, 2009; VanDerHeyden & Burns, 2009). Finally, in relation to behavior, focus is placed on understanding the specific function of the behavior (Iwata, Dorsey, Slifer, Baumann, & Richman, 1982; Mace, Yankanich, & West, 1988).

Frequency

Although research has consistently demonstrated that matching interventions to student skill leads to success, intervention design is at best a hypothesis-generating process. Thus hypotheses need to be developed and changed at a fairly rapid pace, and frequent skill measurement is needed. Data are not collected a particular interval, but are collected when changes in intervention are needed. For example, we may collect data regarding a student's math skills to suggest an intervention, attempt the intervention for 3 to 4 weeks, and then determine that modifications to the intervention protocol are needed. We would then collect additional data to further analyze the problem. We may decide that intervention modifications are needed after 2, 6, 8, or 10 weeks and our data collection system must allow that pattern.

Sensitivity to Change

Screening data can be used to monitor growth over the course of a year, and data used to monitor progress should show growth on a weekly basis, but data used to identify interventions must show immediate changes in behavior. Brief experimental analysis (BEA) is used to systematically and rapidly test the effects of different interventions and intervention components using a within-participant approach (Daly, Witt, Martens, & Dool, 1997). Using BEA, a few selected interventions are tried briefly (e.g., one to three sessions) and then evaluated to see which is most successful. This process allows for an intervention test drive both to see which intervention produces the most desired effect and to collect feedback on intervention fit from the teacher. Several studies have examined the effectiveness of BEA for identifying effective individualized interventions for improving academic skills and behavioral outcomes (Bonfiglio, Daly, Martens, Lin, & Corsaut, 2004; Burns & Wagner, 2008; Noell, Freeland, Witt, & Gansle, 2001), all of which relied on extremely sensitive data that could result in 80% increases in outcome data over the course of one intervention session (Burns & Wagner, 2008). This topic also links to the next point of determining intervention effectiveness, which is essentially an extended analysis of the intervention selected using this stage of assessment.

Determine Intervention Effectiveness

The final stage of any intervention model is to determine the effectiveness of the intervention, which is consistent with a summative evaluation paradigm (Bloom et al., 1971). However, data collected after or during intervention to determine effectiveness can be used for formative purposes by making changes to interventions based on a lack of student growth, and combining effectiveness data with screening and intervention design completes a comprehensive formative evaluation model. Although various measures can inform different aspects of an assessment to intervention model, CBM seems ideally suited to monitor progress for academic issues and direct behavior ratings (DBRs) for behavioral concerns; both of these are discussed in subsequent chapters.

There is considerable research examining the psychometric adequacy of CBM and DBR data when monitoring progress (Ardoin & Christ, 2009; Chafouleas, Sanetti, Kilgus, & Maggin, 2012; Christ, 2006; Riley-Tillman, Chafouleas, Sassu, Chanese, & Glazer, 2008; Riley-Tillman, Methe, & Weegar, 2009; Yeo, Kim, Branum-Martin, Wayman, & Espin, 2011). The reliability of the data depends on the decision being made. If the monitoring data are being used to modify an intervention, then a lower standard (e.g., 0.70 or 0.80) is needed than if the data are being used to make entitlement decisions. Although CBM data are generally sufficiently reliable for most decisions, there are characteristics of the progress-monitoring system that need to be in place for reliable decisions to be made (e.g., at least 8–10 data points; Christ, 2006). The National Center on Response to Intervention rates tools appropriate for monitoring progress when focusing on general outcomes (*www.rti4success. org/progressMonitoringTools*) or specific skills (*www.rti4success.org/progressMonitoring-MasteryTools*). Several monitoring tools are rated on reliability and validity of the scores, but also of the slope of growth and rates of improvement. Several measures meet all criteria for effective progress monitoring, most of which are commercially available CBM packages, and are listed in Table 2.1. As with screening measures, there currently no widely available rating of behavioral progress-monitoring tools. Luckily, the recently funded National Center for Intensive Intervention (*www.intensiveintervention.org*) will soon provide a vetted rating of behavior measures that have evidence to support their use for behavioral progress monitoring.

Precision

There is a need for precision and generality when monitoring progress. Practitioners should use both GOMs and SMMs when evaluating the effectiveness of an intervention. GOMs provide information about progress in the global skills (e.g., reading), but SMMs demonstrate progress or lack thereof in the skill that the intervention is targeting.

An example of the need for both measures comes from the experience of the second author (M.K.B.) while working in a K–2 elementary school. Each month the school team met to examine intervention effectiveness data and to problem-solve any difficulties. One of the special education teachers presented data for all of her students that consisted of oral reading fluency CBMs and were presented in individual graphs. Unfortunately, the data over the previous 4 weeks suggested a flat rate of growth, and the frustrated teacher stated, "I'm doing a decoding intervention, and by the way, Dr. Burns, it is the decoding intervention that you recommended, and my students aren't doing well. What do I do?" We examined the data and concluded that a decoding intervention was probably appropriate based on our intervention-design data, but that not enough time had passed to see an effect in this general measure. We recommended that the teacher still collect the ORF data because they are good measures of overall reading proficiency, but that she also collect data regarding the students' decoding skills. She then started collecting nonsense word-fluency data on a weekly basis in addition to the ORF data, and an immediate growth in skill was noted.

As can be seen from the example above, a skill measure was able to show growth before the general measure did. Thus relying only on GOMs might have resulted in prematurely abandoning an intervention. Alternatively, relying only on SMM to monitor intervention effectiveness would not indicate increases, or lack thereof, in global skills and may result in maintaining an intervention too long when there was a need to further accelerate growth.

Frequency

Data used to monitor progress should be collected frequently. As stated above, research by Christ (2006) found that a minimum of approximately eight data points is needed to make reliable decisions. Thus if data are collected only once per week or less, much more time will be needed to obtain sufficient data to make a reliable decision. Data are often collected weekly, and once every other week should be considered a minimum for effective data-based decision making. If a team wishes to discuss the effect on an intervention after several weeks, an appropriate data collection schedule should be designed. This is one reason why it is critical that progress monitoring measures are designed so that they can be efficiently collected. For example, a CBM probe can only take a few minutes to administer, while DBR probes can take less than a minute for each data point. Different types of data within one progress monitoring system could be collected at different intervals. For example, SMM data could be collected weekly, but well-constructed GOMs such as ORF could be collected every other week, and even more global measures (e.g., an individually administered measure of reading comprehension) could be collected once each month.

Sensitivity to Change

Because the goal of progress monitoring data is to document changes in a target behavior, data used for this purpose must be sensitive to change. Traditional assessment practices are often criticized for a lack of instructional utility because they lack overlap between assessment and curriculum, and are insensitive to changes in behavior. Student performance on norm-referenced tests is interpreted in comparison to a norm group, which makes it difficult to obtain changes in scores between test administrations.

Measures designed for progress monitoring purposes such as CBM and DBR are generally more sensitive to change than most standardized measures used in schools. SMM data are often more sensitive to change than GOMs, but the latter should also be sufficiently sensitive to model short-term growth in the global skill, which again supports the argument for collecting both types of data within a progress monitoring system.

Many measures used to monitor progress are timed (e.g., ORF), and we frequently field questions from classroom teachers about the need to time these measures. Yes, there are legitimate concerns about timing assessments for some students, but there are several distinct advantages. First, timing the measure increases its standardization, which is important if the data are to be used for important decisions. Second, timing the measure makes it much more sensitive to change. Consider two third-grade students who are struggling learning their single-digit multiplication facts. Both students are assessed with the facts for the 3's, 4's, and 6's and are allowed 2 seconds to respond to each one. If the student responds correctly within 2 seconds, then the fact is counted as correct, but incorrect responses or responses given after 2 seconds are counted as errors. There are 10 facts each, for a total of 30. Assume one student has no trouble and correctly states the answer for all 30 within 2 seconds each and completes the task with 100% accuracy in about 28 seconds. The other student also can state the answer for each one, but he must think about it much more thoroughly. The second student correctly answers all 30, but requires 54 seconds to do so. Thus both students have a score of 30, or 100% correct. However, do these two students have the same level of mastery of the problems? The answer is no, and timing the assessment is the only way to determine the difference between the two sets of skills. Moreover, if an intervention helps a student go from completing all 30 facts in 54 seconds to completing all 30 facts in 28 seconds, then those data suggest an effective intervention, which would not be seen in comparing 100% to 100%.

Determine Whether Special Education Is Warranted

Although the focus of multi-tiered system of support is and should be on using data to enhance student learning (Burns & VanDerHeyden, 2006), the application of the construct to an RTI model came from special education identification. IDEIA 2004 allowed schools to use a process that determines whether the child responds to *scientific, research-based interventions* as a part of the evaluation procedures for learning disability (LD) eligibility determination. Data used for LD identification must be held to the highest standards for reliability ($\sim$ 0.90; Salvia et al., 2013) and validity. A review of research, policy documents, and ethical guidelines suggested that RTI-based assessment practices, when carefully implemented, have the potential to be multifaceted, fair, valid, and useful (Burns, Jacob, & Wagner, 2008). However, there were legitimate threats to acceptable RTI-based assessment practices including poor treatment fidelity; a lack of research-based interventions appropriate for diverse ethnic groups, older students, and students with limited English proficiency; and inconsistent definitions of nonresponse to intervention and when that would warrant formal referral for evaluation of special education eligibility (Burns, Jacobs, & Wagner, 2008).

The issues of precision, frequency, and sensitivity are less relevant for this decision than for the other three, partly because the other three decisions happen within the RTI framework and this final one (LD identification) is the result of the process. Thus the precision, frequency, and sensitivity are determined within the different decisions made during the process, and LD identification is not the outcome of the model. In other words, some practitioners in the schools where we work express concern that identifying students as LD with an RTI process will slow down the identification process because they need to attempt a Tier 2 intervention for 8 weeks or so, then a Tier 3 intervention for another 8 to 10 weeks. Unfortunately, this proposed progression reflects a misunderstanding of RTI because LD identification does not happen by starting an RTI process when a difficulty is suspected; it happens by examining the data that already exist. Therefore, the technical adequacy of the model and

> **LD identification does not happen by starting an RTI process when a difficulty is suspected. It happens by examining the data that already exist.**

the data collection procedures should be evaluated within the context of the specific decisions within the model.

IDEIA requires "a full and individual initial evaluation" prior to providing special education services (Public Law 108-466 § 614 [a][1][A]), which could include health, vision, hearing, social and emotional status, general intelligence, academic performance, communicative status, and motor abilities, if appropriate. Collecting RTI data is not in and of itself a comprehensive evaluation, but additional data are collected only when appropriate. According to the 2006 *Federal Register*, U.S. Department of Education personnel stated in the comments section that

> the Department does not believe that an assessment of psychological or cognitive processing should be required in determining whether a child has an SLD [specific learning disability]. There is no current evidence that such assessments are necessary or sufficient for identifying SLD. Further, in many cases, these assessments have not been used to make appropriate intervention decisions. (p. 46651)

Thus comprehensive evaluations for LD identification using RTI data may be determined by appropriate precision, frequency, and sensitivity within the model and not whether cognitive processes were measured. We discuss LD identification extensively in Chapter 9 and discuss evidence-based interventions in Volume 1.

TREATMENT FIDELITY

Valid decision making is the primary criterion by which all assessment data are judged (Messick, 1995). Treatment fidelity has been repeatedly identified as the greatest threat to valid decisions within an RTI model (Burns, Jacobs, & Wagner, 2008; Noell & Gansle, 2006). Consistent and correct implementation of interventions is necessary to assure substantive intervention plans (Noell & Gansle, 2006). The relationship between treatment plan implementation and outcome is complex (Noell, 2008), but generally speaking, treatments become increasingly likely to lose effectiveness or fail entirely as implementation integrity decreases (Gansle & McMahon, 1997; Noell, Duhon, Gatti, & Connell, 2002; Vollmer, Roane, Ringdahl, & Marcus, 1999). It is also worth acknowledging that some omissions in treatment implementation appear to be less critical and that some imperfections in implementation are likely to have little practical consequence (Noell & Gansle, 2006).

Intervention fidelity is a multifaceted construct that should be assessed with multiple sources of data (Sanetti & Kratochwill, 2009). Most assessments of treatment fidelity consist of direct observations of interventions while following intervention protocols to determine whether the steps of the intervention are in place (Sanetti et al., 2011), but that treats fidelity like a unidimensional construct. Instead, a four-pronged approached is recommended that includes examining permanent products, directly observing the intervention, self-monitoring and self-reporting, and using manualized treatments and intervention scripts (Sanetti & Kratochwill, 2008). Using manualized interventions that include intervention scripts could lay the foundation for treatment fidelity assessments because the scripts could be used to judge the permanent products, to observe the intervention, and to complete self-reports. The intervention protocols included in Volume 1 were designed to assist as scripts, or as the basis for scripts to be created, from which implementation integrity could be assessed.

Permanent Product

Perhaps the most basic component of a treatment fidelity plan is to examine permanent products. Just about any intervention that occurs in K–12 schools results in something being created. For example, reading interventions may use student workbooks and assessments, initial placement worksheets, student books, and so forth. Behavioral interventions include products such as completed behavioral reports, markings on a board, and completed token economy sheets. Moreover, computer-based interventions are ideal for examining permanent products because they often include daily or weekly point sheets or can easily record the number of activities completed. Although the presence of permanent products does not ensure that an intervention was implemented with fidelity, the absence of the products suggests an intervention fidelity issue.

Direct Observation

Intervention scripts can be easily converted into implementation checklists with which practitioners can observe interventions. Although there is no research-based minimum, integrity checks generally involve observing 20–25% of the intervention sessions. This may be an unrealistic goal in an applied setting, and using a multidimensional approach reduces the required frequency with which the interventions must be observed, but 10% seems to be a reasonable minimum expectation. If these checks are random and unscheduled, they are logically more likely to accurately estimate typical levels of implementation integrity.

Perhaps it is more important to ask how much integrity is needed, rather than how often interventions should be observed. It seems that 90% integrity would assure effective implementation, but that is not always the case. For example, if a teacher were to implement a behavior plan that involved reinforcing alternative behavior, which was observed with a 10-item checklist for which providing the reinforcement was one item, then 90% integrity would not be sufficient if the one item that was not observed was the actual provision of the reinforcement. Therefore, intervention teams are encouraged to discuss (1) how often the observation should occur, (2) what is the minimum level of implementation integrity that would be judged as sufficient, and (3) what items are most critical to success. One of the components of the intervention briefs is Volume 1 is related to this issues. Those briefs presented "critical components" for each intervention. In terms of integrity checks, those critical components must be present for integrity to be considered sufficient. Ideally, all interventions will be presented in this manner over time to help educational professionals know what elements are essential and what elements can be altered.

Self-Report

Previous research found that teachers can accurately self-report treatment fidelity (Sanetti & Kratochwill, 2009). Thus intervention protocols can also be used as a self-report implementation checklist in which the teacher reports whether each aspect of the intervention plan was implemented. Once again, there is no hard-and-fast rule about how often self-report should occur or how much integrity is needed. Self-report data can be easy to collect, but it adds another requirement to the implementer. Thus self-report data may be collected only periodically, such as weekly, but brief self-reports could be collected daily or at every intervention session.

Implementation Integrity System

Implementation integrity is important, but does not happen by accident, and neither does the assessment thereof. School-based teams must carefully design a process for assessing integrity while initially developing the intervention and intervention plan. Sanetti and Kratochwill (2009) described a three-stage process in which teams first define the intervention and the necessary steps within it, then collaboratively plan the integrity assessment plan, and finally create a self-assessment from the information included in the previous phases. This process should be implemented at various levels of the RTI process.

Grade-Level Teams

In our experience, many schools start the RTI implementation process by starting a problem-solving team (PST). We can promise that if your first step in implementing an RTI framework is to start a PST, then your model will be doomed to failure. PSTs are a powerful aspect of an RTI model, but have two shortcomings. First, as we discuss below, most PSTs do not solve problems—they admire them. Second, starting a PST as the first step likely ignores the most important point. On average, 20% of students require more assistance than they receive in a typical general education curriculum (Burns, Appleton, & Stehouwer, 2005). Consider an elementary school of 500 students. If a PST meets to discuss any students experiencing a problem, then they will meet to talk about 100 students (20% of 500 = 100), which is far too many to conduct an in-depth analysis and to implement individualized interventions. Instead, schools are wise to start by examining the quality of the core curriculum. Thus it is not the PST that drives an RTI process, it is the grade-level team (GLT).

We discuss effective GLTs in Chapter 6. For this conversation we will assume GLTs meet to discuss Tier 1 difficulties, to identify who needs Tier 2 interventions, and to evaluate the progress of students receiving Tier 2 and Tier 3 interventions. See below for discussion about schools without GLT. We suggest that GLTs meet on a weekly basis to discuss Tier 1 and Tier 2 interventions and that they identify two types of evidence for the interventions. First, the outcome data should be discussed to determine how they will assess progress and student learning. Second, they should identify process goals in order to monitor the progress with which the instructional activities or interventions are implemented, and at that monthly meeting they develop an implementation integrity assessment plan.

Table 2.2 lists the phases of the intervention assessment plan and how a GLT could implement it. Permanent products for instructional activities can consist of items like student workbooks, but could also include lesson plans and student assessments. We also frequently record instructional lessons in order to view and discuss the lesson at future GLT meetings.

The GLT team also evaluates student progress and implementation integrity associated with Tier 2 interventions. Most commercially prepared interventions appropriate for Tier 2 include some sort of implementation checklist that the team can adopt and convert into a self-report assessment. Moreover, we (Burns, Deno, & Jimerson, 2007) examined research to determine the components of an effective Tier 2 intervention and created a generic obser-

TABLE 2.2. Example of an Intervention Integrity Assessment Plan for GLTs at Tiers 1 and 2, and PSTs at Tier 3

	Phase 1: Define intervention	Phase 2: Develop a plan	Phase 3: Self-assessment plan
GLT instructional lesson (Tier 1)	Teachers select the activity and determine essential components.	Teachers collaboratively determine permanent products (e.g., lesson plans) and find implementation checklists (e.g., curriculum guide or protocols).	Teachers determine what will be discussed at next GLT meeting.
GLT small-group intervention (Tier 2)	Teachers select the intervention and determine essential components.	Teachers collaboratively identify permanent products from the intervention (e.g., student workbook), and create or find an intervention protocol.	Teachers convert intervention protocol into a self-report and determine how often each aspect of the integrity plan will be implemented. The data are shared at each subsequent GLT meeting.
PST interventions and PST process (Tier 3)	PST identifies intervention and essential attributes.	PST ends every meeting by deciding what will serve as a permanent product, of what the intervention protocol will consist, and how the interventionist will self-report. PST also identifies a checklist for the PST process and selects the essential items from it.	Interventionist completes the self-report and all data are reported back to the PST at the follow-up meeting. The PST ends each meeting by deciding whether they implemented the four or five items from the PST process implementation checklist that they judged to be most important. The PST decides whether they implement all of the items from the PST process implementation checklist on a periodic basis.

vation checklist that is available in Form 2.1, at the end of this chapter. Team members could also identify permanent products within the intervention protocol at the monthly GLT meeting. If the intervention is not commercially prepared, then the GLTs would have to identify the essential components of the intervention, develop an intervention protocol, and convert that protocol to a self-report.

It is important to address schools without GLTs. For example, small rural schools may have one teacher per grade. Another common example is at the middle- and high school level, where there may be department teams rather than GLTs. In such situations some group should commonly meet to fill the GLT role. It is impossible to outline a model that will work for every school, but we do feel that once the role of GLT is understood, a good principal can apply those responsibilities to a logical team of educational professionals.

Problem-Solving Team

The RTI process is driven by the GLT, but a high-functioning PST is critically important for developing interventions within Tier 3 after reviewing relevant data from Tiers 1 and 2. Thus, the PST should (1) identify the intervention, (2) decide how progress will be monitored, (3) determine what permanent products will be created, (4) select or create an intervention protocol, (5) convert the intervention protocol to a self-report, (6) determine how often each integrity assessment will occur, (7) write the intervention integrity assessment plan into the intervention plan, and (8) examine the integrity plan data at a follow-up consultation and at the follow-up meeting.

In addition to intervention integrity, the integrity with which the problem-solving process was implemented should be examined. Burns, Peters, and Noell (2008) created a 20-item checklist and used it to provide performance feedback to the team. Simply providing performance feedback increased the integrity with which the items were implemented. However, some important items were not implemented (e.g., develops an intervention plan with the teacher). Thus the PST should identify four or five items that take priority. They could be items that the team judges to be most important, or they could be items that the team judges to be weaknesses for that particular team. Then the PST would judge whether they implemented those four or five items at the end of every meeting, and would periodically complete the entire checklist (e.g., once a month, once a quarter, once a semester). The self-report implementation data should be stored somewhere as documentation that the PST process occurred.

CONCLUSION

RTI can be conceptualized as the use of assessment data to systematically and efficiently allocate resources for the purpose of improving learning for all students (Burns & VanDer-Heyden, 2006). Thus those of us who are passionate about assessment see this as an opportunity to finally use school-based assessment data to their fullest potential. We know what data are needed in order to conduct assessment *for* learning (Stiggins, 2005), and we know how those assessments should be conducted and the data used within a multi-tiered system of support. Data should be used to identify who needs additional intervention, what intervention is needed, to determine whether the intervention is effective, and to determine whether special education services are needed. However, data for these important decisions will not lead to valid conclusions within an RTI framework unless the interventions are implemented with fidelity, which is assessed with the combination of permanent products, direct observation, and self-report.

> Data should be used to identify who needs additional intervention and what intervention is needed. Then, data will determine if the intervention is effective and if special education services are needed.

Effective data collection efforts and treatment fidelity are keys to successful RTI implementation. In subsequent chapters we discuss specific data to examine at Tiers 1, 2, and 3 to answer the questions outlined in this chapter, and we discuss personnel who should examine the data and the process to do so. All of these factors combined lead to multi-tiered systems of support that address the learning needs of all students.

Generic Tier 2 Fidelity Observation Checklist

Item	Observed	
The Tier 2 intervention is:		
1. Implemented or supervised by a qualified teacher with reading expertise	Yes	No
2. Targeting one specific reading skill	Yes	No
3. Targeting a skill that is consistent with one of the five areas identified by the National Reading Panel	Yes	No
4. Implemented 3 to 5 times/week	Yes	No
5. Implemented in 20- to 30-minute sessions	Yes	No
6. Delivered in a small-group format	Yes	No
7. Occurring in addition to core reading instruction	Yes	No
8. Designed to last at least 8 weeks	Yes	No
9. Monitored with a rate-based measure and slope of student reading growth	Yes	No
10. Evidence based (at least a moderate effect size)	Yes	No

From T. Chris Riley-Tillman, Matthew K. Burns, and Kimberly Gibbons (2013). Copyright by The Guilford Press. Permission to photocopy this form is granted to purchasers of this book for personal use only (see copyright page for details). Purchasers can download additional copies of this form from *www.guilford.com/riley-forms*.

CHAPTER 3

Assessment for Problem Solving

Assessment is the foundation for RTI, for interventions in general, for special education, and for quality instruction. As stated in Chapter 2, we see RTI as a systematic use of data to allocate resources in order to enhance student outcomes. There are heated debates regarding quality instruction for math and reading, from which the only point of general consensus is that assessment is critical to the process (National Mathematics Advisory Panel, 2008; National Reading Panel, 2000). However, there is some debate as to what type of data are most useful (Batche, Kavale & Kovaleski, 2006).

As stated in Chapter 2, many have proposed that data from measures of cognitive processing help inform the intervention process, but multiple meta-analyses have questioned that claim (Burns et al., 2012; Kavale & Forness, 1999). Instructionally relevant data should indicate on what specific skills more time should be spent, which students are adequately progressing, and the appropriate instructional match for each student (Afflerbach, 2007; August, Carlo, Dressler, & Snow, 2005; Sweet & Snow, 2003). This framework applies to both academic and behavioral difficulties. We focus on the role of all assessment in RTI in this chapter, but we present academic and behavior assessments together rather than break this discussion into two sections because the very point of each is to facilitate the problem-solving approach.

PROBLEM-SOLVING FRAMEWORK

There is some debate about the origins of RTI, but in our opinion it can be most directly traced to Deno and Mirkin's (1977) *Data-Based Program Modification* (DBPM) manual, which operationalized a problem-solving model for identifying and responding to student learning problems. Stan Deno is the "godfather of RTI," but not for reasons that many would think. CBM is commonly used within an RTI framework, which we discuss below, and CBM was developed by Deno and colleagues at the University of Minnesota (Deno, 1985). However, CBM was developed as just a tool to be used within a problem-solving framework (Fuchs & Deno, 1991). In fact, the Deno and Mirkin (1977) document is often credited as giving birth to CBM, but the term *curriculum-based measurement* does not appear anywhere in that book. Instead, the DBPM manual was the first articulation of an educational application of a problem-solving process, which was the construct from which RTI was born. In that book Deno and Mirkin outlined not only the problem-solving process that would in time become RTI, but also identified the need for assessment methods to support such a process.

The term *problem solving* describes any set of activities designed to "eliminate the difference between "what is" and "what should be" with respect to student development" (Deno, 2002, p. 38). Deno's seminal work relied on the IDEAL problem-solving model: (1) Identify the problem, (2) Define the problem, (3) Explore alternative solutions to the problem, (4) Apply a solution, and (5) Look at the effects of the application (Bransford & Stein, 1984). In a recent chapter, Deno (2013) outlines assessment using the IDEAL problem-solving model. Burns and colleagues (2007) suggested that the IDEAL problem-solving model could be the framework around which a unified RTI model could be created. There

> The term *problem-solving* describes any set of activities designed to "eliminate the difference between "what is" and "what should be" with respect to student development.

must be flexibility in designing RTI models for individual schools because each school is a unique system. However, each RTI model should place problem solving at the core, and schools should build their framework around it. Note that all stages of this model assume that some method of collecting data fuels the problem-solving process. Unfortunately, in the 1970s and 1980s, such assessment approaches/tools were not available.

As noted throughout this book, RTI models generally operate around three tiers of intervention (Marston, 2003), and problem-solving activities occur within each. Tier 1 is generally quality core instruction and schoolwide behavior management, Tier 2 is a targeted intervention for a small portion (e.g., 20%) of the population, and Tier 3 is individualized interventions for an even smaller portion (e.g., 5–10%) of the student population. It seems that many practitioners conceptualize the difference between the tiers based on the size of the group. For example, Tier 1 is classwide instruction, Tier 2 is small-group instruction, and Tier 3 is one on one. However, we frequently operate interventions within Tier 3 that are small group and also deliver Tier 2 interventions in a one-on-one format. What differen-

> What differentiates the three tiers is not the size of the group, but the level of analysis needed to determine the intervention and the resources needed to deliver it.

tiates the tiers is not the size of the group, but the level of analysis needed to determine the intervention and the resources needed to deliver it. A thorough understanding of the level of analysis, and the type of data necessary to support such analysis, is critical for RTI to work.

PROBLEM ANALYSIS

Problem solving occurs within each tier, but each successive tier involves more in-depth analysis than the previous one in order to determine which intervention is appropriate. The primary problem analysis question for each tier is listed in Table 3.1.

As can be seen in the table, data are collected more frequently (three times per year in Tier 1 to weekly assessments for Tier 3), and data are collected more precisely as students progress through the tiers. This process of collecting data more frequently and precisely is conducted so that school-based teams can engage in more in-depth problem analysis. The first question involves low-level analyses and can be answered with screening data. However, multiple data sources are needed to address the analysis question for Tier 2, and functional data are needed for Tier 3 to identify a causal relationship. Below we discuss the problem-solving process within each tier of intervention, with a focus on problem analysis, and discuss appropriate measures of academic skills to conduct that analysis.

Although we made this point briefly in Chapter 2, we feel the need to reinforce it here. The primary problem analysis questions for Tiers 1 and 2 are answered by GLTs and PSTs do not become involved in the RTI process until a Tier 3 intervention is needed. Problem-analysis questions within Tiers 1 and 2 are addressed with screening and instructional data that are owned by most GLTs, and minimal expertise is needed to address these questions. However, Tier 3 data are highly specific, and considerable expertise is needed to interpret them. Thus a multidisciplinary team with advanced training is needed for Tier 3, but might unnecessarily slow down the process in Tiers 1 and 2. Moreover, resources for intensive individual assessment should be reserved in Tiers 1 and 2 in order to use them in Tier 3.

TABLE 3.1. Primary Problem Analysis Questions for Each Tier

Tier	Analysis question	Data that address the problem	Frequency of data collection
Tier 1	Is there a classwide problem?	Screeners (e.g., CBM, Measures of Academic Progress, STAR Reading and STAR Math, Office Discipline Referrals, Direct Behavior Ratings)	Data are collected three times per year for screeners. Data collected as part of a process (e.g., ODR, attendance) will be continually available.
Tier 2	What is the category of the problem?	Combinations of general outcomes measures and specific skills	Skills are diagnostically assessed on a periodic basis and progress is monitored at least twice each month.
Tier 3	What is the causal variable?	Highly sensitive data to show a functional relationship	Diagnostic data are collected periodically and progress is monitored at least once each week.

PROBLEM ANALYSIS WITHIN THE TIERS

Tier 1

Identify the Problem

The first step in the problem-solving framework is to identify a problem, which is usually accomplished by comparing current student performance with what is expected (Deno, 2002). Perhaps the essential attribute of Tier 1, beyond quality core instruction, is universal screening. The schoolwide skill level is screened three times each year. Some may read this and wonder why only three assessment times are sufficient, when certainly classroom teachers collect data far more frequently than that. We hope that is true, but in order to efficiently allocate resources to enhance student learning, we only need to assess student skills three times. Moreover, our assessment of student skill is not very rich; all we need is universal assessment three times per year in conjunction with classroom assessment if each student reads at grade level (or completes math computation, behaves appropriately, etc.).

Because screening is not an in-depth process, general outcome measures (GOMs) work quite well. Jenkins (2003) described the following attributes of an effective screening model:

1. It accurately distinguishes individuals who require intervention from those who do not.
2. It is practical, which suggests that it be brief and simple to administer but also result in reliable data.
3. The use of the data to screen students results in a positive net effect (e.g., avoids inequitable treatment, does not consume resources that could be put to better use, and is directly linked to effective interventions).
4. The data can be integrated with assessments used in other parts of an RTI model.

While discussion of GOMs typically focuses on academic skills, this concept is also quite effective for social behavior (Chafouleas, Riley-Tillman, & Christ, 2009). Using traditional behavioral ideology, a GOM is an estimate of the presence of a behavior cusp that, when exhibited, allows for the opportunity for other activities. For example, learning to drive allows an individual to greatly expand the places they can go. In relation to education, when a child learns to behave in a classroom environment and academically engage, they then have the opportunity to learn in a classroom setting. This is similar to when a child learns to read fluently, which opens up the opportunity to learn from reading.

Define the Problem

Identifying who needs help is only the first step. Next, the GLT examines the data to analyze the problem, but these analyses in Tier 1 do not typically rely on additional data. In Tier 1, the problem is usually defined by comparing an individual student's score to a criterion and then determining how discrepant the score should be to identify a problem.

However, there are two other considerations. First, the question of classwide problem must be addressed using only the screening data that are collected and comparing those data to a criterion. We discuss this is some detail in Chapter 6. Second, even the best assessment system is going be correct only 90% of the time, which suggests that there is opportunity for error in 10% (or, more realistically, 20%) of the decisions. It may be helpful for teachers to compare all screening data to classroom assessments to make sure the results align. This process can catch data entry mistakes or other anomalies that need to be checked with a rescreen for a small number of students.

Most of the decisions regarding who needs additional support can be made with screening data alone. However, GLTs should then "examine the margins" to be sure that no students are missed. We discuss this in more detail in Chapter 6, but our point here is that additional data may be needed to be certain that no students fall through the cracks. We suggest that GLTs consider additional evidence for students who score slightly above the criterion score. For example, at Kreucher Elementary, all second-grade students are screened with ORF three times each year, and all students who read fewer than 25 words correct per minute in the fall are identified as needing a Tier 2 intervention. There are approximately 100 second graders in four classrooms at Kreucher Elementary, and 20 of them had an ORF score of 25 or less in the fall. However, two students in Mr. Schafer's room had ORF scores of 28 and 29. Thus Mr. Schafer would bring additional data to inform the discussion about these two students. He may bring standardized assessments given only to individual students (e.g., spelling inventories), informal assessments for individual students (number of sight words correctly read from a grade-level list), or he may bring samples of student skill taken from activities in which all students engage (e.g., partner reading and comprehension questions). GLTs would be wise to discuss the types of data needed to inform this decision so that they are consistent and so that the decision is always made with data.

Explore Alternative Solutions

Because the level of analysis is low in Tier 1, the choices of interventions should be narrow, and the decision should rely almost solely on the screening data. Certainly GLTs could look for patterns in classroom data such as spelling inventories or math tests and use those data for instructional remediation. For example, if a spelling inventory suggests that many students in the grade struggle with *r*-controlled vowels, or math tests indicate common difficulty with two-digit by two-digit multiplication with regrouping, then the GLT may decide to reteach those skills. In the case of behavior, the identification of clusters of general behavior issues can highlight where more attention should be provided to classroom management. In the case of a spike of office discipline referral in a specific class,

> **Because the level of analysis is low in Tier 1, the choices of interventions should be narrow, and the decision should rely almost solely on the screening data.**

GLTs could work with a target teacher to reteach class rules or examine the environment for alteration in prompts (e.g., posting of rules and procedures). The process of using data to drive instruction and classroom management is simply effective teaching, which is certainly part of an RTI model but is not specific to resource allocation. To efficiently allocate resources to enhance learning for all students, we need to assess "can read/can't read," "can do math/can't do math," "can behave/can't behave," and so on, three times each year, and those decisions can be made with screening data. We discussed interventions for Tier 1 extensively in Volume 1, and will not repeat that discussion in this book.

Look at Effects of the Application

As is the case with other phases of problem solving for Tier 1, screening data are sufficient to allocate resources and monitor progress. The data collected three times each year are sufficient to determine whether the students are making adequate progress. However, if a classwide problem is found (see Chapter 6), then progress should be monitored more frequently. We have found that every other week seems to be sufficient a rule of thumb, but we base that on experience more than research. If a classwide problem is noted, then the same general outcome measure used to screen the students is administered every other week to monitor progress. If the screener is a tool that cannot be administered every other week (e.g., a group-administered test of comprehension), then it is probably best to administer a CBM such as ORF, maze, or single-digit computation probes, or a formative behavior rating such a direct behavior ratings.

Tier 2

Identify the Problem

Problem identification for Tier 2 overlaps with decisions made within Tier 1. Screening data are used to identify classwide problems and to identify students who need additional support. The students who score below the predetermined criterion are identified as needing a Tier 2 intervention, but as stated above, those who fall slightly above or below the criterion should be considered as well, and additional data should be brought into the conversation.

Define the Problem

Problem analysis within Tier 2 is somewhat more detailed than Tier 1 and involves additional data. The primary problem-analysis question for Tier 2 is "What is the category of the problem?" In Chapter 2 we defined GOMs and subskill mastery measures. Thus far in this chapter we have focused on GOMs because they are excellent sources of data for screening decisions. However, subskill measures are very important to finding the category of the problem within Tier 2. Once the GOMS indicate that there is a difficulty, skill measures can then be used to isolate it.

> **The primary problem-analysis question for Tier 2 is "What is the category of the problem?"**

The category of the problem for reading relies on the so-called Big Five of the National Reading Panel (2000), in which reading is composed of phonemic awareness, phonics, fluency, vocabulary, and comprehension. Math is not as clear in that the structure does not fit into similarly specific areas. Thus single-skill probes of grade-level standards are important, and are discussed more in Chapter 6. We also believe it is critical to include behavior in the discussion. Similar to the Big Five for reading, we argue that there are three critical behaviors that children need to exhibit in order not to be considered as having "behavior problems." Specifically, behavior success is composed of academic engagement, respectful interactions, and a lack of disruptive behavior (Chafouleas et al., 2009; Riley-Tillman, Chafouleas, Christ, Briesch, & LeBell, 2009). Specific observation of these behaviors and the antecedent and consequence of the behavior should foster an understanding of the behavioral concern. Table 3.2 lists areas for academic and behavioral difficulties that should be examined and some potential general assessment ideas for those areas. As described in Chapter 1, the data used for these decisions do not have to be as reliable as for other types of decisions. Thus some teacher-made tests may be sufficient to determine the category of the problem, but a combination of various CBMs (e.g., ORF for reading fluency and nonsense-word fluency for decoding) can also provide a relatively clear starting point for intervention.

TABLE 3.2. Skill Measures for Various Subskills within Academic and Behavioral Difficulties

Reading	Math	Behavior
Phonemic awareness • Phoneme segmentation • Rhyming • Phoneme blending	Computation • Single-skill computation probes	Academic engagement • Actively or passively participating in the classroom activity.
Decoding • Spelling tests and inventories • Pseudoword/nonsense words • List of decodable but low-frequency words	Conceptual understanding • Problems with abstract items • Interview about process to solve items	Nondisruptive behavior • The absence of student action that interrupts regular school or classroom activity.
Fluency • ORF with grade-level text	Problem solving • Word problems • Application problems	Respectful behavior • Compliant and polite behavior in response to adult direction and/or interactions with peers and adults.
Comprehension • Questions after reading		

Explore Alternative Solutions

Once the analysis is done to identify the category of the problem, an intervention menu should be used to select the intervention. For example, in the case of a minor behavior problem where a student is disruptive in order to obtain teacher attention, an intervention such as Check In–Check Out can be quickly selected from a menu of behavioral interventions for use with attention-seeking children. Tier 2 still involves relatively low-level analysis and should be conducted by GLTs with rather minimal training. A sample menu of interventions was included in Volume 1 and criteria to interpret the categorical data is included in Chapter 7.

Look at Effects of the Application

As intervention selection in Tier 2 is conducted quickly and with limited data, it is understood that success is by no means assured. Only after the intervention is conducted do we have evidence to support that it was indeed evidence based for the specific child or group of children. Unfortunately, monitoring progress is a critical but often forgotten aspect of the intervention process. CBM was explicitly designed to monitor progress precisely because Deno and Mirkin (1977) pointed out the need to use sensitive data to determine the effectiveness of an intervention. Thus GOMs such as ORF are excellent data to monitor progress and should probably be administered at least every other week. However, if the intervention will focus on a specific skill, then progress in that skill should be monitored as well. For example, if a student is receiving a decoding intervention, then progress should be monitored at least every other week with a decoding-based measure (e.g., nonsense = word fluency). If the intervention addresses multiplication facts, then the measure should also address that skill. In relation to behavior intervention, DBR was developed to fill a similar role to what CBM provides for academic intervention (Chafouleas et al., 2009). Using DBR teachers can efficiently and accurately rate children's specific target behavior to document the effectiveness of behavior interventions. We suggest monitoring academic progress at least every other week with both a skill and GOM. In Tier 2, it may be appropriate to monitor progress every week, but alternating on a weekly basis between a skill and GOM. For behavior, it will be important to document multiple times a week, as behavioral performance tends to be more highly variable. As such, it is important to use methods that are highly feasible.

Tier 3

Identify the Problem

Identifying the problem within Tier 3 is somewhat controversial. For example, some have advocated that students be identified as needing a Tier 3 intervention with screening data in which CBM scores at or above the 25th percentile would be considered within the average range and suggest that universal instruction alone (Tier 1) is most appropriate; students with scores within the 10th to 25th percentile are identified as at risk and receive a Tier

2 intervention; and those below the 10th percentile demonstrate severe needs and participate in a Tier 3 intervention (Shinn, 2005). This makes intuitive sense, though, because students who have the lowest scores have the largest gain to make up in order to close the gap between expectation and performance. However, recent meta-analytic research found that preintervention CBM data (and other types of data as well) do a very poor job of predicting who will respond well to specific interventions (Burns & Scholin, 2012). Thus using preintervention data to triage students might result in substantial waste of precious school resources.

It might be best to start most students with a Tier 2 intervention and make changes quickly for the lowest-performing students. However, that does not mean that *all* students start at Tier 2 and that no one ever receives a Tier 3 intervention without first going through Tier 2. Instead, students are only rarely placed directly into a Tier 3 intervention, and the decision is made with data. Teachers should bring classroom data with them to the GLT meeting in which seasonal (fall, winter, spring) screening data are discussed, and those data should be used to identify who needs a Tier 3 intervention. Assessments of phonemic awareness are particularly helpful for reading, math concepts for math, and disruptions for behavior. Thus problem identification in Tiers 1 and 2 can be made with screening data, but problems in Tier 3 should be identified through multiple sources of data.

Define the Problem

The primary goal within Tier 3 problem analysis is to hypothesize about the causal variable, or the environmental variable that is both malleable and directly related to the problem. Certainly there are child-centered attributes that affect student learning, such as aptitude and attention span, but those are not variables that we can control. Instead, assessments to determine Tier 3 interventions involve in-depth analyses of environmental and instructional materials. Moreover, data used to define the problem within Tier 3 must be especially sensitive because they must show immediate change in performance or lack thereof.

Data used to analyze the problem within Tier 3 are collected by the school's PST. Most decisions made within Tiers 1 and 2 rely on low-level analysis for which minimal training is needed. However, a much more functional approach is needed for Tier 3, and much more training is usually required than what most classroom teachers receive. Thus we suggest that at least two people in the building receive advanced training on problem solving, functionally analyzing data, and the PST process. We suggest two highly trained individuals so that if one leaves, there is still someone to provide this critical support. Ideally, a core cadre of school professionals also receive training in these areas to create a strong PST. They should receive advanced training in the basic procedures of functional analyses and in one or more specific frameworks to analyze behavioral and academic difficulties. Pathways for such advanced training are discussed in Chapter 9.

Curriculum-based evaluation (CBE; Howell & Nolet, 2000) is a problem-analysis procedure that was used successfully among some early RTI models (Ikeda et al., 2007). A variety of assessments can be used within CBE, including CBM and various subskill mastery measures (SMMs). Perhaps the essential attribute of CBE is the use of a curriculum map that shows the order in which various subskills and strategies are taught, which are then sequentially assessed with SMMs to determine where a student requires additional intervention (Hosp & MacConnell, 2008). To adequately describe CBE would go beyond the scope and sequence of this book, and the research base for CBE is not well developed. Readers are referred to several excellent book chapters by Howell and colleagues (Howell, 2008; Howell, Hosp, & Kurns, 2008; Kelley, 2008) for more information. The review, interview, observe, test/instruction, curriculum, environment, and learner (RIOT/ICEL) matrix is also associated with RTI Tier 3 problem analyses and is discussed below.

There are several problem-analysis approaches with a more well-developed research base that can be used to make decisions about interventions within Tier 3, including Gickling's model of curriculum-based assessment for instructional design (CBA-ID; Gickling & Havertape, 1981), the instructional hierarchy (Haring & Eaton, 1978), and five hypotheses for student failure (Daly et al., 1997). Below we discuss each of these frameworks, but start with a succinct discussion of functional analysis in general as the basis for Tier 3 problem analyses.

FUNCTIONAL ANALYSES

There is a long line of research supporting the effectiveness of functional analysis of problem behaviors to define the problem for children with severe behavioral and academic difficulties (Iwata et al., 1982; Mace et al., 1988; McComas, Hoch, & Mace, 2000; McComas & Mace, 2000), all of which relied on CBM or systematic direct observation (SDO). While it is beyond the scope of this book to provide a comprehensive overview of functional behavior analysis (FBA), it is important for the construct to be understood. Functional analysis is composed of two related steps. First, through a variety of methods (interview, observation, and assessment) a hypothesis is generated as to why a child is exhibiting a specific problem behavior. Typically, there is a common set of functions with associated interventions that have been documented to be effective. For example, a team might hypothesize that a child is calling out in class to gain adult attention. Volume 1 of this book contained a detailed framework for intervention selection based on function. There we outline how academic problems can typically be grouped into acquisition, proficiency, and generalization categories. We used a similar framework for behavior problems with increased specificity in the proficiency category to focus on behaviors based on a desire to escape something, or behavior based on a desire to gain something.

The second stage of FBA is the analysis stage, where the hypothesized intervention is tried in a manner that can test whether the function was selected correctly. In the case of the child who was hypothesized to be misbehaving to get teacher attention, an evidence-based intervention such as noncontingent reinforcement in the form of teacher praise could be implemented. If the child's misbehavior decreases we would have support that the function of the problem behavior is attention seeking. Chapters 4 and 5 in this book provide a detailed overview as to how schools can implement interventions to support functional analysis.

RIOT/ICEL

Another framework that is currently used to analyze problems for a Tier 3 intervention is referred to as the RIOT/ICEL matrix. RIOT stands for *Review Interview, Observe,* and *Test,* and represents sources of assessment data. ICEL stands for *Instruction, Curriculum, Environment,* and *Learner,* and represents areas to be assessed. The PST first examines a student's problem and makes at least two hypotheses for each area (ICEL). They then place those within the RIOT framework to determine how those areas should be assessed (Hosp. 2008).

Table 3.3 is a sample RIOT/ICEL matrix for a hypothetical third-grade student who successfully completes math work during instruction, but who does not accurate complete independent work. A hypothesis is generated for each of the four areas (ICEL), and assessment strategy to test each hypothesis is planned for each assessment domain (RIOT). Therefore, this framework allows the school's PST to systematically test each hypothesis, and interventions are derived based on the ones that are confirmed.

TABLE 3.3. Sample RIOT/ICEL Matrix

	Review	Interview	Observe	Test
Instruction *Hypothesis*: Student needs more repetition during instruction to recall later.	Examine previous work to determine type of errors.	Interview student about why he or she makes mistakes.	Observe student while working independently.	Provide more repetition to see if it improves accuracy.
Curriculum *Hypothesis*: Directions for independent work are not clear.	Examine previous work to determine type of errors.	Interview student about directions.	Observe student while reading directions.	Assess the accuracy with which student reads directions.
Environment *Hypothesis*: Student is distracted by what is around him during independent work.	Examine previous work to determine type of errors.	Interview student and teacher about environment during independent work.	Observe environment while working independently.	Assess student's on-task behavior while working independently.
Learner *Hypothesis*: Student does not recall the math facts without support.	Examine previous work to determine type of errors.	Interview teacher about math fact knowledge.	Observe student to determine strategies used during independent work.	Assess retention of math facts before beginning independent work.

CBA-ID

CBA-ID is an intervention design method framework that uses assessment to identify a match between student skills and instructional material (Gravois & Gickling, 2008). Academic skills are sampled for short durations (e.g., 1 minute) and are compared to instructional-level criteria. An instructional level is reached when the student can complete tasks with minimal assistance (Gickling & Thompson, 1985), which equals 93–97% of the words read correctly for reading and 85–90% items correct for other tasks such as math facts, spelling words, letter sounds, and sight words (Burns, 2004; Gickling & Thompson, 1985).

The assessment material for CBA-ID consists of the instructional material. In other words, reading is assessed with the reading curriculum materials, math with math assignments, spelling with spelling lists, and so forth. Specific procedures to conduct a CBA-ID are the following:

1. Students are presented with a sample of the instructional curriculum. For reading, the instructional material could consist of a page from the reading basal, a graded passage used for repeated reading, or some other sample of connected text. However, younger children may receive a list of sight words, or letters to generate letter sounds. The stimulus for math is likely going to be a single-skill probe based on the skill being taught in the classroom (e.g., single-digit multiplication). Math stimuli could simply be samples of homework or other independent practice.

2. Students are instructed to perform the task for 1 to 2 minutes. For reading, they orally read the passage/page for 1 minute, in math they silently complete the task for 2 minutes, and sight words and letter sounds are completed orally for 1 minute. There is nothing magical about 1 minute, except that data obtained from 1 to 2 minutes are sufficiently reliable for decision making (Burns, Tucker, Frame, Foley, & Hauser, 2000), but you do not gain much reliability or instructional utility by going beyond 1 or 2 minutes.

3. After completing the timing, the number of items (words for reading, sight words, letter sounds, etc.) correctly completed are counted. The CBM scoring procedures rely on digits correct per minute for math and letter sequences for spelling. For example, the three problems below would have six digits correct possible, rather than just three problems, and this example would result in five out of six (83%) correct digits.

$$
\begin{array}{ccc}
4 & 3 & 4 \\
\times\ 4 & \times\ 5 & \times\ 6 \\
\hline
16 & 18 & 24 \\
\end{array}
$$

The following examples for writing would be scored with correct letter sequences. The word *house* would not be scored as one correctly spelled word, but as six correct letter sequences of space to *h*, *h* to *o*, *o* to *u*, *u* to *s*, *s* to *e*, and *e* to space. While counting a space in a list like this seems confusing, it makes more sense in contextual spelling, and so the student should be given credit for putting the h first and the e last. In the example below, the student would receive 15 out of 17 (88%) because they received full credit for the first two, but only for space to *t*, *t* to *o*, and *n* to space. The *o* to *w* sequence was incorrect, as was the *w* to *n* sequence.

> *h o u s e*
>
> *m o u s e*
>
> *t o u n (town)*

4. The percentage successfully completed would then be compared to an instructional-level criterion of 93–97% for contextual reading, and 85–90% for most other skills.

CBA-ID data have limited generalizability to the broader construct (e.g., reading), but they indicate the likelihood that a student will successfully interact with a given text or set of instructional materials. Students who read less than 93% correct (i.e., the frustration level) are likely to be discouraged and often exhibit behavioral difficulties such as off-task behavior (Gickling & Armstrong, 1978; Treptow et al., 2007), and those who read more than 98% of the words correctly are often not sufficiently challenged.

Some practitioners examine errors per minute during reading and math and compare the data to instructional level criteria. Deno and Mirkin (1977) suggested that three to seven errors per minute while reading represents an instructional level, but errors per minute are meaningless data. In other words, it is impossible to interpret the number of errors made while reading in 1 minute unless the assessor knows the total number of words read or total number of items completed. For example, assume that a student reads 50 words per minute with five errors, which converts to 90% correct. Assume, then, that after an intervention a student reads 80 words per minute but continues to make five errors, which is 94%. The student's accuracy has improved, but the errors per minute remains the same. Moreover, two students could read with five errors in 1 minute, which represents an instructional level according to Deno and Mirkin, but one student may have made those errors while reading 20 (75%) words and one while reading 50 (90%) words. In this example, the same score represents two very different skill levels.

From a problem-analysis perspective, CBA-ID can be extremely useful because the data can suggest a potential source of student frustration. For example, if a student is reading fewer than 93% of the words correctly, or completing fewer than 90% of the math problems correctly, then she is likely experiencing frustration that will result in decreased learning and potential behavioral difficulties. To consider what this is like think about reading a book where you don't know 1 in every 10 words. Very few people would persist with reading such a book. When students are performing at a frustration level, then more appropriate material can be used. Recent research has found large effects on behavior and student learning when specific unknown items were pretaught before instruction (Burns, 2007). Moreover, CBA-ID data are sufficiently reliable for instructional decision making (Burns et al., 2000; Burns, VanDerHeyden, & Jiban, 2006).

INSTRUCTIONAL HIERARCHY

The instructional hierarchy (Haring & Eaton, 1978) is an analysis framework that, as we suggested in Volume 1, could provide the basis for many types of behavior analyses. Essentially, the hierarchy provides a method for matching interventions to a child's skill proficiency to produce the strongest gains for the student. We proposed that this hierarchy applies regardless of the skill being taught, which included social behavior.

The instructional hierarchy includes the four phases outlined in Table 3.4: (1) acquisition, (2) fluency, (3) generalization, and (4) adaptation. As shown in the table, students in the acquisition phase complete tasks slowly and inaccurately. That is the child who has no idea how to begin a task or how to behave when presented with a social situation, which requires that the student be given explicit instruction with high modeling and immediate feedback. After a child can perform the task accurately, but slowly, then he or she is functioning in the fluency phase. That is the child who can perform the task, but really has to think about it (e.g., reading one sound at a time, completing math by counting on fingers). Children in the fluency phase require independent practice. However, independent practice for children in the acquisition phase may actually be counterproductive; until a child can perform a task accurately, we do not care how quickly he or she can perform it.

Generalization is the application of newly learned information to situations other than those in which the skill was learned (Alberto & Troutman, 2006), and is critical to the learning process. Students cannot generalize a skill until they can perform it with sufficient speed and accuracy. Thus students proceed from the fluency phase into the generalization phase once they are both accurate and fluent in the task, which then requires guided practice in different materials and providing cues to support generalization. Finally, once a student can generalize the new skill then she can use the information to solve problems (adaptation).

TABLE 3.4. Instructional Hierarchy Phases of Learning and Subsequent Interventions

Stage of learning	Student proficiency	How do you know?	Goal of intervention	Intervention example
Acquisition	Frustration	Responses are hesitant and incorrect	Establish 100% correct	• Modeling • Guided practice • Immediate corrective feedback
Fluency	Instructional	Responses are accurate but slow	Build fluency	• Timed performance with incentives • Delayed feedback • Goal setting • Fading of reinforcement
Generalization and adaptation	Mastery	Responses are fluent	Establish robust application	• Guided practice applying skill to solve more complex problems • Variation of task materials • Cues or prompts to generalize

The learning hierarchy can be used to determine interventions by assessing the accuracy and fluency with which skills are performed. If a student does not complete the task accurately (e.g., reading fewer than 93% of words correctly, answering fewer than 90% of math facts correctly, correctly responding when cued 60% of the time), then tasks associated with the acquisition phase (e.g., modeling, explicit instruction, and immediate feedback) should be selected as the core of intervention. However, a student who is accurate but still slow requires independent practice in the skill.

HYPOTHESES FOR STUDENT FAILURE

Daly and colleagues (1997) proposed the following five hypotheses for why students fail: (1) insufficient motivation, (2) insufficient practice, (3) insufficient feedback and assistance, (4) insufficient modeling, and (5) materials that are too difficult. These five hypotheses also provide a potential framework to analyze a problem. However, each is only a hypothesis that would have to be directly tested, usually in a brief experimental approach described below.

SUMMARY

These analysis frameworks are not mutually exclusive in that a CBA-ID could certainly be conducted within a RIOT/ICEL framework or to test the hypothesis that the task is too difficult. The research base for CBE and RIOT/ICEL is not as strong as it is for Daly's five hypotheses, CBA-ID, or the learning hierarchy. However, which analysis framework is selected is not as important as selecting one, training the PST on the framework, consistently using it, and measuring fidelity of its use.

Explore Alternative Solutions

Once the problem is analyzed, specific interventions should be suggested and briefly tested. Brief experimental analysis (BEA) is a common method to quickly test the relative effects of two or more interventions on a target behavior (Daly et al., 1997), which allows practitioners the opportunity to "test drive" the intervention (Witt, Daly, & Noell, 2000) in approximately the same amount of time needed to complete a standardized measure of achievement (Jones & Wickstrom, 2002). School-based personnel manipulate environmental or instructional variables within a BEA by implementing a series of interventions and assessing the immediate effect on a particular outcome. The intervention or combination of multiple interventions that leads to the largest gain is then implemented.

There is a decade of published BEA research that demonstrated positive effects for reading fluency (Burns & Wagner, 2008), math (Carson & Eckert, 2003), spelling (McComas et al., 1996), writing (Duhon et al., 2004), and behavior problems (Carter, Devlin, Doggett, Harber, & Barr, 2004; Wacker, Berg, Harding, & Cooper-Brown, 2004). However, relatively few school psychologists receive training in BEA (Chafouleas, Riley-Tillman, & Eckert, 2003). We discussed the procedures for conducting a BEA elsewhere (Riley-Tillman & Burns, 2009), but briefly do so below.

The first step in a BEA is to select the interventions to be tested. Although BEAs can test the relative effectiveness of any intervention or combination of intervention components, the system with which they are selected is an important aspect of the analysis. For example, the five hypotheses outlined by Daly and colleagues (1997) could be directly tested by comparing interventions such as (1) a contingent reward (insufficient motivation), (2) repeated reading (insufficient practice), (3) immediate error correction (insufficient feedback and help), (4) listening passage preview (insufficient modeling), and (5) using materials that represent an instructional level based on CBA-ID (materials that are too difficult).

Next, each intervention is briefly administered in a predetermined order both to gauge their effectiveness and allow for the interventionist to have an opportunity to try out administration (Noell et al., 2001; VanAuken, Chafouleas, Bradley, & Martens, 2002). Experimental control in a BEA is demonstrated by using a multi-element design (Eckert, Ardoin, Daisey, & Scarola, 2000; Eckert, Ardoin, Daly, & Martens, 2002; Noell et al., 2001) or a brief multi-element design followed by a mini-reversal with baseline or the least successful intervention (Daly et al., 1997; Daly, Martens, Hamler, Dool, & Eckert, 1999).

The results of BEA will suggest which intervention is the most effective, and this in turn can give insight into what is causing the difficulty. For example, if contingent reward led to the largest effect, then we could conclude that the child likely has acquired the skill and is unmotivated to complete it. Interventions could then be developed based on this information that would have a higher likelihood of effectiveness than just randomly selecting any intervention.

Apply a Solution

Once interventions for Tier 3 are found to be effective for an individual student, they are implemented over an extended period. Interventions selected within Tier 3 can be highly individualized and should address a highly targeted deficit. Tier 3 interventions were addressed in depth in Volume 1.

Look at Effects of the Application

As is the case for Tier 2, CBM and DBR seem ideally suited to monitor progress for individual students within Tier 3. Data collected to monitor progress can be collected less frequently for Tier 2, but both skill and GOM data should be collected at least once each week for students getting a Tier 3 intervention. In fact, it may be advantageous to collect CBM or DBR data multiple times each week.

WHAT ABOUT THE 50 OTHER THINGS THAT NEED TO BE ASSESSED?

As noted throughout this chapter, data are the fuel for the RTI engine. While there are clearly a number of outcomes such as reading fluency and academic engagement that have been validated for use in a problem-solving model, far more outcomes have received little attention in practice or research (e.g., high school content areas, reading comprehension). If RTI models are to succeed, methods must be available for schools to address all target outcomes. Rather than wait the years (if not decades) it will take for a full portfolio of methods to be developed and validated for use in a problem-solving mode, we strongly suggest that educational professionals return to 1977 and consider the problem facing Deno and Mirkin. They needed assessment methods to fuel their operationalized problem-solving model, and set about developing CBM. Likewise, any educational professional should feel empowered to consider what tools they have on hand to provide data relevant to their problem-solving needs. Weekly spelling tests, end-of-chapter tests, or data from a classroom token economy all present the opportunity for contextually relevant formative outcome data sources. Such measures could be used as such as long as they are collected as part of a specific problem-solving framework like the ones described here. Considering that such measures will not have the research base to document their psychometric properties, teams should be careful not treat them as precise measures of the outcome. Regardless, if used with a grain of salt and implemented in a consistent manner, measures like the weekly spelling test can help a PST make data-based decisions. Perhaps the influence of Deno and Mirkin will extend to the schools and result in a wave of school-based measures with utility for a schoolwide problem-solving process.

CHAPTER 4

Evaluating Interventions
Applied Single-Case Design

WHAT IS APPLIED SINGLE-CASE DESIGN AND WHY IS IT IDEALLY SUITED FOR RESPONSE TO INTERVENTION?

As discussed in Chapter 1, SCD is a class of experimental methods that have been designed to demonstrate the relationship between an independent variable (typically called the intervention) and a dependent variable (e.g., time on task or ORF data) in a single "case" (e.g., student or classroom). SCD has a long history as a core research method in a variety of fields with thousands of published studies using this approach. Simply put, SCD is a tried-and-true experimental approach ideally suited for use in educational settings.

Before moving on to discuss the basics of SCD, two questions should be addressed. First, why do we need an experimental approach when using RTI? This question has been generally addressed in Volume 1, and in Chapter 1 in this book, but it is worth the time to review prior to jumping into why SCD is the preferred experimental approach. RTI is based on linking the appropriate intervention with the case at hand. While it would be ideal if we could give the child a simple test and know how to intervene, evidence-based practice is not that simple. Evidence-based interventions (EBIs) are developed to work with specific problems (e.g., an attention-seeking child or a child with low levels of accuracy in reading text). Once developed, EBIs are validated in a series of studies that essentially show that they are effective on average across a group of participants. While it would be wonderful to find an EBI that was universally effective, the complex environment of a classroom and the dynamic relationship between a teacher and student(s) results in EBIs being those that, when selected and implemented correctly, have an attractive probability to result in the desired outcomes. As a result, it is critical that when we use EBI, we incorporate procedures to assess the outcomes to document that, for a particular case, we have evidence that the EBI is effective. In the end, we consider an intervention to be evidence based for a specific child/situation when it has been shown to be effective for that child/case. While in many cases simply documenting that an intervention is effective for a specific case is sufficient, in some cases it is also important to determine whether the intervention is responsible for the desired outcomes. This last sentence is rather important. There are many situations in schools where it is fully acceptable to stop at the determination that an intervention of some sort is "successful." If a child is responding to schoolwide positive behavior interventions and supports (SWPBIS) as documented by no office discipline referrals, then we can say that the child is being successfully supported at that level of intervention. It is irrelevant whether the child is actually responding to SWPBIS, or whether the child would act appropriately in almost any regular classroom environment. As continuing a child in Tier 1 is the common practice for all children who don't exhibit academic or behavioral issues, we don't need to know exactly why the child succeeded. On the other hand, if a school were to decide to use an intensive approach for a student which pulled him from his classroom for 50% of the day, then it would be critical to have data to support that the intervention, and only the intervention, was responsible for desired outcomes. Given the restrictive nature of that intervention, it would be unethical to continue use without ample evidence that the intervention indeed was responsible for the observed outcome. This level of assurance can only be developed by adopting an experimental approach. SCD is essentially the only experimental method that can be feasibly used in educational environments.

Once the importance of adopting an experimental approach is established, the next step is to select an approach that is compatible with the school environment. If you were to pick up a copy of any academic journal focusing on school psychology or special education, you would see that most of the studies tend to compare a group that gets the intervention with another group that does not. Using this approach has proven to be quite effective to produce results that can be generalized to other students similar to those in the studies. Unfortunately, this approach is not well suited for application in schools for several reasons. First, few teachers could run a group design study and still complete their teaching responsibilities. Second, it is not ethical in a school to fully withhold a treatment from a group of children just to see if it works for other children. Third, and perhaps most important, in school intervention cases we are not often interested in a group of children. Rather, we are interested in how a specific child responds to an intervention. This is simply not what this class of experimental design was created to examine. In contrast, when a single child or case is the target, SCD is the ideal choice of research methodology. By adhering to an appropriate SCD, researchers or educational professions can determine the impact of interventions (independent variables) on outcome data (dependent variables) with only one student or case. How this is accomplished is outlined below in the section on baseline logic. An additional advantage of SCD is that it is very flexible. With an understanding of the basics of SCD, an educational professional can design a variety of approaches. This flexibility makes it more likely that there will be an appropriate design for each situation. In the end, SCD and analysis was developed in a manner that makes it the ideal experimental approach for educational professionals who seek to make defensible educational decisions in an RTI model.

BASICS OF SINGLE-CASE DESIGN: BASELINE LOGIC

Prior to considering specific single-case "designs," we believe it is essential for educational professionals to fully understand the underlying experimental logic. As noted above, if you understand how and why designs are created you can use designs in a much more flexible manner and recognize the implications of changes that occur in applied settings. "Baseline logic" (Cooper et al., 2007; Johnston & Pennypacker, 1980; Sidman, 1960) is the experimental logic with which specific designs have been created. Before we proceed into specific aspects of baseline logic we should note that we make one alteration to the typical three-step baseline logic model (Cooper et al., 2007). To make the model more useful in applied setting, we use a four-step model in this book (Riley-Tillman & Burns, 2009; Riley-Tillman & Walcott, 2007). Specifically, we have included the first intervention trail (described below as *affirmation of the consequent*) as a specific step. This diverges from traditional models, as affirmation of the consequent is typically considered only a form of replication (Sidman, 1960). Although it will be apparent that such replication is critical in demonstrating a relationship between the intervention and the behavior of interest, in applied work the first demonstration, while understood to be nonexperimental, can also be quite important. Specifically, our model of baseline logic is composed of four steps: (1) prediction, (2) affirmation of the consequent, (3) verification, and (4) replication by affirmation of the consequent.

Prediction

In any intervention case we start with some problem behavior, and the general goal of the intervention process is to change that behavior in some defined manner. As such, it is necessary that the behavior be understood and measured sufficiently so that any change can be recorded. Given this starting point, the first phase of baseline logic is to determine and record the salient features of the behavior before attempting EBI. In baseline logic this stage is called "prediction." The prediction phase builds on the assessment processes described in the preceding chapters.

The collection of baseline data allows for three aspects of the problem-solving process. First, such data allow a more refined understanding of the problem behavior. As discussed in Volume 1, minor differences in the problem behavior can have an impact on the correct intervention pathway. The second use of baseline data is aligned more to the analysis phase than the intervention selection phase. A sufficient stream of baseline data allows documentation of how the target behavior is naturally changing in the absence of a defined EBI. This is particularly important in schools, as often our goal is to increase the rate of learning rather than teach a fully novel skill. Understanding the current level, trend, and variability of a target behavior will be critical as we consider the goals for intervention, and subsequently whether those goals were realized. Due to this goal, formative data that display changes over time in a target behavior is more desirable than a static single data point (e.g., standardized test score), which can't document change. Finally, baseline data allow us to ask "Did the intervention work?" Without knowing exactly where the child's academic or social behavior started, one can never say whether the intervention had an effect. As such, it is critical to collect enough baseline data to provide a full understanding of the target behavior, as represented in the outcome data prior to the implementation of an EBI. In the absence of this information, there is simply no pathway to measure a child's response to intervention.

With each stage of baseline logic, it is useful to consider the actual statement made by the phase. For the prediction phase the statement is as follows:

> If we do nothing, this is what we can expect the child's behavior to look like in the future.

With a sufficient and steady stream of outcome data it is possible to predict future behavior assuming that nothing changes (Cooper et al., 2007). Figure 4.1 displays a baseline-phase data path and the predicted outcome data, assuming no intervention changes. Clearly, there is a problematic assumption in this phase in that it is assumed that nothing changes after the baseline phase has ended. Educational environments are complex and rarely static. Rather, new tactics are often being tried out with children. Any of these tactics could alter the target behavior. For example, changes in curriculum can affect curricular match (become too hard or too easy) and influence both on-task behavior as well as academic progress (Treptow et al., 2007). As such, the prediction statement is understood to be tentative and in need of

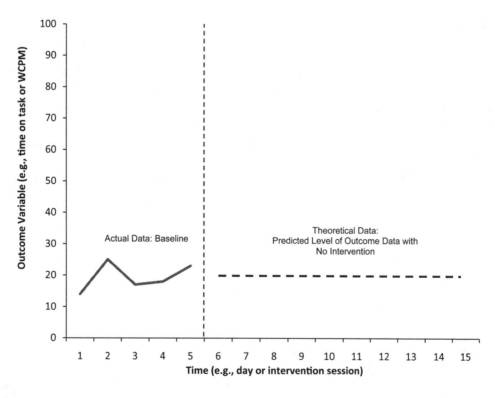

FIGURE 4.1. Baseline logic: Prediction. From Riley-Tillman and Burns (2009; adapted from Cooper, Heron, and Heward, 2007). Copyright by The Guilford Press. Reprinted by permission.

verification if one is to put a significant amount of stock into it. In an attempt to strengthen the predication statement two steps can be taken. First, the more data collected the stronger the predication statement. While we discuss this issue in more depth in the next chapter, at this stage it is sufficient to say that data collected over several days are preferable to data collected in one day. The longer the duration and the more data points collected, the better one can understand the preintervention environment. Second, steps should be taken so that in the baseline-stage interactions with the child are as close to "business as usual" as possible. The more "typical" teachers, parents, and other educational professionals can be with the child when collecting baseline data, the more useful the information will be for subsequent analysis. To accomplish this task it is critical that all involved understand both the importance of baseline data and the procedures to collect high-quality baseline data.

In our experiences, when pressed many educational professionals have a difficult time explaining the importance of measuring preintervention behavior. In light of this it is important for the rationale for this phase to be sufficiently explained to teachers or other educational professionals who will use SCD. We find the ideal guiding question is "What happens if we don't establish a defensible prediction statement?" With a bit of discussion it is clear that in the absence of the predication statement, a child's response to the intervention cannot be established, as a team can never say with confidence that the behavior has changed. Without knowing where you started, you can't argue that you are in a new place.

Affirmation of the Consequent

After the prediction statement has been established, educational professionals have the opportunity to try the intervention and observe the effect. Technically, establishing baseline data allows for the first test of the hypothesis that the selected EBI will have a desired impact on the target behavior. We call this phase "affirmation of the consequent" to highlight some problems with the first intervention trial. This phase is based on two assumptions, both of which, frankly, are problematic (Riley-Tillman & Burns, 2009):

> **Technically, establishing baseline data allows for the first test of the hypothesis that the selected EBI will have a desired impact on the target behavior.**

1. If nothing is done, the target behavior as represented by the outcome data will remain stable.
2. If the intervention is functionally relevant to the target behavior, then there will be some predictable change in the outcome data after implementing the intervention (Cooper et al., 2007; Johnston & Pennypacker, 1980).

We discussed the issue with the first assumption above when reviewing the prediction phase. As for the second assumption, any student in an undergraduate Logic 101 course would recognize that this as a classic formal fallacy called affirmation of the consequent (Audi, 1999; Runes, 1942). The logic outline of affirmation for the consequent is as follows (Riley-Tillman & Burns, 2009):

If *X*, then *Y*

Y

Therefore, *X*

The experimental adaptation of this is:

If the independent variable is a controlling factor for the dependent variable (*X*), then the outcome data will show a change when the independent variable (*Y*) is present (if *X*, then *Y*).

The outcome data show a change when the independent variable is present (*Y* is true). Therefore, the independent variable is a controlling variable (effective in changing) for the dependent variable (therefore, *X* is true).

The educational intervention adaptation of this is:

If the intervention is a controlling factor for the behavior (*X*), then the data will show a change when the intervention (*Y*) is present (if *X*, then *Y*).

The data show a change when this intervention is present (*Y* is true). Therefore, the intervention is a controlling variable (effective in changing) for the behavior (therefore, *X* is true)

The fallacy in any of the above statements rests on the reality that there could have been other reasons than *X* that *Y* occurred. While *X* results in *Y*, it does not mean that it is the *only* condition that can change *Y*. For example, consider the following:

If you have food poisoning, you will feel nauseated.

You feel nauseated.

Therefore, you have food poisoning.

While food poisoning could be the reason for the nausea, there are other possibilities. For example, if alcohol was concurrently consumed, that could result in nausea. Or this could be a case of the flu. Any time someone contracts an illness that involves nausea there was some food consumed in rather close proximity that had nothing to do with the illness. In the case of research or applied intervention there should be an attempt to control as many other relevant variables as possible. In other words, the only change implemented at the time of intervention should be the intervention. Unfortunately, even in the most rigorous experimental situations it is understood that there are always unknown variables that could account for the observed outcome.

In Figure 4.2 you can see a graph describing affirmation of the consequent. The baseline data predict that the child should continue in the range of 15–25% on task unless some

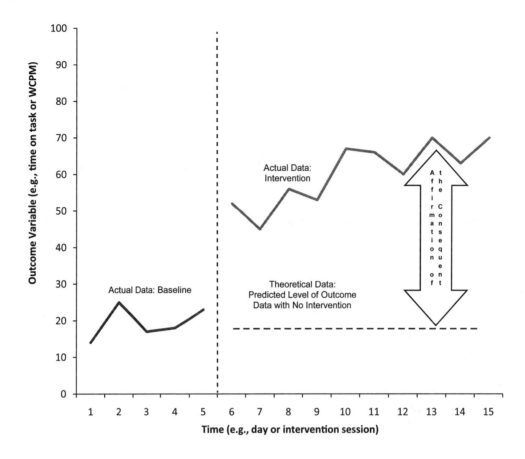

FIGURE 4.2. Baseline logic: Affirmation of the consequent. From Riley-Tillman and Burns (2009; adapted from Cooper, Heron, and Heward, 2007). Copyright by The Guilford Press. Reprinted by permission.

intervention in attempted. When the intervention is applied, the consequent of the prediction statement is observed. Specifically, the child does not continue in the range of 15–25% on task, but rather immediately increases to more than 50% on task, and then continues to increase on-task behavior while the intervention is in place. This first observation of the intervention effect starts to build a case that the intervention is effective. Of course, without subsequent manipulation we don't know whether it was the intervention or some other variable responsible for the observed change. Verification and replication will address this weakness.

Stepping back, it is important to ask what you know after the first observed affirmation of the consequent. As a researcher, any initial finding is highly tentative and will be followed up by subsequent steps to increase confidence about the relationship between the independent and dependent variables. Without these steps no causal relationship can be suggested after this first observation. Considering that this book is not intended for traditional researchers, the case of applied educational research is more relevant. Whereas causal statements are of the utmost importance for traditional researchers, they may be less important for a single educational case. In most cases in the schools, it is probably sufficient to document that the child is getting better, and future performance projection is based on the current performance. If a child is demonstrating a trend that will catch her up to relevant peers, then most educational professionals will be satisfied. Essentially, we don't really need to know whether the intervention caused the desired change. The first affirmation of the consequent allows us to achieve this level of analysis and as a result is quite important for applied practice. In some cases, though, particularly when using a child's response to intervention to make a high-stakes decision (e.g., labeling the child LD) it does become essential to consider the causal relationship between the intervention and the outcome behavior. We go into depth about using RTI for eligibility determination later in the book, but there are two primary pathways for determining special education eligibility for students. In some cases a child will not respond, or not respond enough, to interventions across Tiers 1, 2, and 3. Such a child would then be referred for special education services. In other cases, schools using RTI may label a child due to a response to a highly intensive intervention at Tier 3. Logically, this child did not respond to prior less intense interventions. This is the preferred pathway for eligibility determination using RTI, as the intervention approach is understood when the child enters special education. In such a case, it would be unacceptable to label a child due to a response to an intervention when in reality it was unknown whether the intervention was responsible for an observed effect. There are other advantages of establishing a causal relationship. Specifically, establishing that the intervention truly worked allows for one to suggest more strongly the subsequent use of the intervention for the child. If long-term intervention planning is important, then establishing a causal relationship should be considered. In either case (high-stakes decisions or desire for long-term programming) the following two steps of baseline logic become essential.

Verification

Returning to the issues noted in the prediction phase, the primary concern was that predicting that baseline levels of the behavior would continue will eventually be incorrect. Specifically, at some point something would happen to change the target behavior outside of the intervention. To deal with this issue the verification phase was developed. The statement made in the verification phase is as follows:

> In order to strengthen the prediction statement it is verified by again observing the target behavior in the absence of the intervention.

The specific goal of the verification phase is to collect data in absence of the intervention to strengthen the initial prediction (Cooper et al., 2007). Another simple way to describe this phase is that the goal is to "verify the prediction statement."

Although there are several ways to verify a prediction statement, the purest example is to remove the intervention and continue to observe the target behavior. This concept will apply to both academic and behavioral interventions. In this case, if the prediction statement was correct, the behavior should return to the baseline level or, in the case of academic intervention, to the baseline rate of learning. If this occurs, the original prediction statement is greatly enhanced. For example, consider a case where escape-maintained disruptive behavior reduced from a mean of 10 times a day in the prediction phase to once a day in the intervention phase after an antecedent EBI was applied. If the intervention is removed and the level of disruptive behavior returns to 10 times a day, the prediction will be verified.

Figure 4.3 extends our intervention example to add the verification phase with a return to a nonintervention condition typically referred to as "return to baseline." When the intervention is removed, the outcome data change to a level consistent with what was observed in the baseline phase. This provides evidence that the prediction statement is verifiable and that (1) it is reasonable to suggest that the target behavior would have persisted at baseline levels in the absence of intervention and (2) the increase in on-task behavior was likely linked to the intervention. In the absence of verification it seems probable that some other variable is controlling the outcome data. If the intervention is not in place and the change is sustained, then what supports the change in on-task behavior? That question is problematic.

One clear issue with the verification phase in applied educational work is that many interventions in general, and almost all academic interventions, are designed to result in skill acquisition. In such cases it is unlikely that the child will forget everything learned when the intervention is removed. There are two methods to deal with this issue. First,

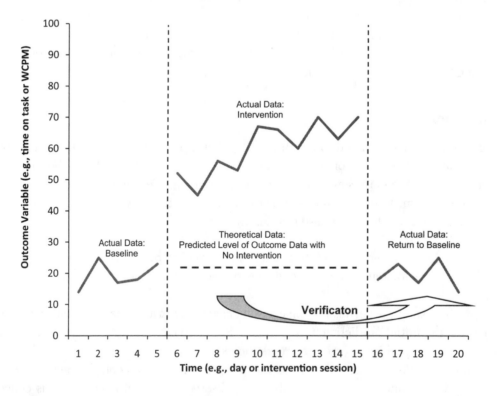

FIGURE 4.3. Baseline logic: Verification. From Riley-Tillman and Burns (2009; adapted from Cooper, Heron, and Heward, 2007). Copyright by The Guilford Press. Reprinted by permission.

while the level of the target behavior is not likely to drop when the intervention is removed, the rate of learning should change. A return to the original trend observed in the prediction phase can be used to verify the prediction statement. A second path is to use more complicated designs (e.g., multiple baseline designs) to verify the prediction through systematic replication. Both of these possibilities are addressed more fully in the next chapter (considering trend in the verification phase) and later in this chapter (multiple baseline designs).

Replication by Affirmation of the Consequent

The final stage of baseline logic addresses the need for replication in order to strengthen our confidence in the initial observation of an intervention effect. The purest version of accomplishing replications is by repeating the intervention after it was removed in the withdrawal phase. Assuming the verification phase was completed successfully, then the target child will be displaying baseline-"like" outcome data. As such, reintroducing the intervention will replicate the initial affirmation of the consequent phase.

Figure 4.4 completes the baseline logic example to demonstrate all of the phases. In this example, the successful replication of the intervention effect reduced the chances that the change in target behavior observed in the second phase of baseline logic (affirmation of the consequent) was the result of something other than the intervention. Technically, the

---

BOX 4.1. Is Withdrawing the Intervention an Ethical Dilemma?

It is fair to ask whether it is unethical to remove an intervention that appears to be working in an attempt to document intervention effectiveness. To briefly end an intervention that seems to be working is simply not a typical approach in most schools. Before discussing this issue, we should break this down into two cases. First, in a case of a severe behavior problem (e.g., self-injurious behavior) it is clearly unethical to remove an intervention that seems to be working in a typical educational setting. For such cases, there are more complex methods that can be used to simulate the verification phase if needed. In most cases, though, the academic or behavior problem will be less severe. In such cases of minor or moderate problem behavior or academic difficulty, the opportunity to remove the intervention can be made on a case-by-case basis. As we discuss in depth later in the chapter, there is little reason in Tier 1 or the early stages of Tier 2 to remove an intervention. At that level, there is no little need to truly know that an intervention is working, as the stakes are quite low. However, in some cases it will actually be more ethical to briefly remove the intervention for verification purposes. When a school discovers an effective intervention, the crisis of the case decreases, and it is typical for the child to receive less subsequent attention. While follow-up assessment should be conducted, there will be other children who will naturally get the bulk of the team's attention. If this is the case, then it is important to know that the intervention actually is working. After the team's attention is shifted away, it could be weeks if not months before the team realizes that the child still struggling. As such, continuing an intervention that is not actually working is really wasting valuable time that could be better used to help a child in need. In the end, the decision to use a withdrawal phase must be made on a case-by-case basis, based on the severity of the case and the importance of understanding the effectiveness of the intervention.

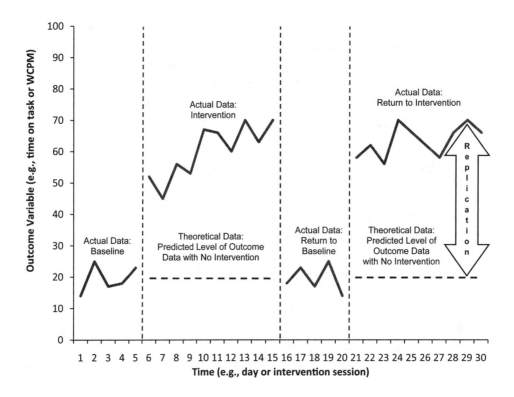

FIGURE 4.4. Baseline logic: Replication by affirmation of the consequent. From Riley-Tillman and Burns (2009; adapted from Cooper, Heron, and Heward, 2007). Copyright by The Guilford Press. Reprinted by permission.

replication phase of baseline logic increases our confidence that the intervention is functionally related to the behavior of interest (Cooper et al., 2007; Riley-Tillman & Burns, 2009).

Although the first replication of the intervention effect increases our confidence in the relationship between the intervention and the behavior, we should not suggest that such a demonstration "proves" the effectiveness of the intervention. Likewise, the lack of replication should not immediately be used as proof that the intervention is ineffective. In schools where there are many changes occurring, there could be several factors that either support or limit the intervention effect. Intervention teams should consider the intervention effect (either positive or negative) and alter the course of action in a manner that best aids the child.

WHY USE BASELINE LOGIC IN APPLIED PRACTICE?

As we conclude the overview of baseline logic and move to discussing traditional single-case "designs," it is worth considering the relevance of the underling philosophy for educational professionals. To be fair, understanding baseline logic may be more complex than simply identifying a design (e.g., A-B-A-B) and applying that in schools. Although we agree that traditional designs are the preferred option, there are several reasons why such an approach often is not reasonable in schools. First, the resources necessary to mount traditional SCD are not available in most educational settings. Consider the differences between an experimental and an applied setting. In a research environment there are typically few cases, a lenient schedule, highly trained staff, and significant research-related resources. In an applied setting there is a massive caseload, pressure to make changes quickly, few trained individuals in SCD, and limited intervention-related resources. In the end, researchers work in settings designed to support research behavior while educational professionals are in environments not suited for traditional research practice.

Second, the requisite level of experimental control needed for many cases in applied settings does not demand fully experimental designs. In research settings, any case where experimental control is suspect is likely to be ignored by researchers. Although those cases might inform future work of the researcher, they are highly unlikely to be published. As publication is one of the primary outcomes of the research enterprise, nonexperimental approaches are avoided by those who wish to remain in the industry. In contrast, most cases in schools don't require experimental control. If a child is responding in Tier 1, it does not ultimately matter whether it is due to the curriculum or to some other factor (e.g., parent tutoring, superior ability, a dynamic teacher). Such a child is considered a Tier 1 success and moves along with his peers until something changes. Likewise in the early stages of Tier 2, if a child responds after receiving a small-group intervention, understanding the role of the intervention is not essential. The child moves back into Tier 1 to progress with his or her peers. Only when practitioners start to use individual intervention does documentation of experiment control creep into the picture. In the end, most cases in schools don't require traditional designs developed to document experimental control. This does not mean that SCD has no place in Tier 1 and 2, as nonexperimental and quasi-experimental models can be highly useful at the whole-school, small-group, and individual levels. Unfortunately for practitioners, quasi- and nonexperimental approaches are not often highlighted in SCD presentations. In that vein we review three such models (B, A-B, and A-B-A) later in this chapter.

Finally, the stakes of an individual case are much higher in applied settings than in research studies. As noted, researchers are interested in cases that can document experimental control, allowing for the relationship between the intervention and outcome to be considered. Cases with violated designs are typically discarded. While this works for the researcher, no case can be thrown away in applied settings. Each applied case is important. As a result, although researchers can ignore a case when a design is violated, practitioners are forced to pick up the pieces and learn what they can from the failed design. This is where a post hoc analysis of the design using baseline logic comes in handy. Considering which (if any) phases of baseline logic have been demonstrated allows you to document what you know and don't know from the case at hand. Table 4.1 was developed to assist with this process. Using this table, consider whether a prediction statement was established, the first affirmation of the conse-

> **Considering which (if any) phases of baseline logic have been demonstrated allows you to document what you know and don't know from the case at hand.**

TABLE 4.1. Questions to Ask to Know You Can Deduce from an Applied SCD

Question	If yes . . .	If no . . .
Were sufficient baseline data collected so that a defensible *prediction* can be made regarding the likely outcome if nothing is done?	It is possible to judge the effectiveness of a subsequent intervention.	It is not possible to judge the effectiveness of a subsequent intervention in a defensible manner.
Has the *affirmation of the consequent* been documented?	Assuming that the prediction step of baseline logic has been followed, this is evidence of response to intervention, although another variable may have caused the observed change.	Assuming that the prediction step of baseline logic has been followed, this is evidence of a lack of a response to intervention.
Was the baseline prediction *verified*?	This supports the prediction statement and makes conclusions about the effectiveness of the intervention more defensible. However, it doesn't preclude that some other variable caused the change as opposed to the intervention.	This weakens the degree of certainty about the effectiveness of the intervention.
Was the affirmation of the consequent *replicated*?	This strengthens the affirmation of the consequent and makes the final conclusion about the effectiveness of the intervention highly defensible.	This weakens the final conclusion about the effectiveness of the intervention.

Note. From Riley-Tillman and Burns (2009). Copyright 2009 by The Guilford Press. Reprinted by permission.

quent was observed, and so on. Although this process will not magically fix a violated design, it will allow for a thoughtful analysis. For example, if the prediction and affirmation of the consequent phases were established successfully but verification did not happen, the case can still document whether there was a change. Such a case cannot document whether observed change can be tied to the intervention, but that may or may not be critical. In the end, in applied settings each case must be used as it can be for the system to keep running.

RELEVANT FORMAL DESIGNS

While a through understanding of baseline logic prepares educational professionals to evaluate intervention outcome data, it is useful to consider formal designs as well. Designs such as A-B-A-B and multiple baseline have been utilized for decades in the research community. As a result, these designs are thoroughly understood in terms of inherent strengths and weakness. A comprehensive overview of formal SCD is beyond the scope of this chapter, but we review A-B-A-B and multiple-baseline designs to provide a starting point for educational professionals. These two designs are the most likely candidates for use in schools, and should provide a solid foundation. Individuals who are interested in a deeper exploration of SCD should consider reading *Evaluating Educational Interventions: Single-Case Design for Measuring Response to Intervention* by Riley-Tillman and Burns (2009).

The ABC Notation System

Prior to discussing typical designs, the "ABC" notation system (Tawny & Gast, 1984) needs to be briefly reviewed. This coding system assigns a letter to each general phase, allowing for designs to be described with short letter combinations (e.g., A-B-A-B or B-A-B) rather than a lengthy verbal overview (e.g., baseline–intervention–baseline–intervention). In addition, the ordering of the letters and dashes allows for complex combinations of interventions. The most common aspects of the ABC coding system are outlined in Table 4.2. By using the ABC coding systems, both simple and complex designs are easily labeled. Table 4.3 provides some sample designs using ABC notation with descriptions.

The Classic "Withdraw" Design

To introduce a withdraw design it makes sense to return to baseline logic. By stepping through each phase of baseline logic, we naturally build into a fully experimental design.

Prediction—Intervention (AoC)—Verification—Replication by AoC
  (A)   (B)   (A)   (B)

TABLE 4.2. Overview of the Basic Codes in the ABC Notation System

ABC code	Condition
A	Baseline condition
B	Intervention condition
C, D, etc.	Subsequent different interventions
B^1, B^2, etc. Or B', B'', etc.	Minor alterations to the intervention
-between letters (e.g., A-B or A-B-B)	A change in phase
Two conditions presented together (e.g., BC)	Two interventions introduced concurrently

TABLE 4.3. Examples of ABC Codes for Interventions, with Associated Descriptions

ABC code	Description
A-B	Baseline phase followed by an intervention
B	Ongoing intervention
A-BC	Baseline phase followed by a phase that is composed of two concurrent interventions
A-B-A-B	Baseline phase followed by an intervention, a return to baseline, and then reintroduction of the same intervention
A-B-BC	Baseline phase followed by an intervention and then a phase with the first intervention and a new intervention applied concurrently
A-B-B	Baseline phase followed by an intervention and then a phase with an altered version of the first intervention (e.g., increased dosage)

This design started with a phase in which the target behavior is measured until a prediction can be made. This phase is followed by introducing the intervention, which allows for the first demonstration of the intervention effect (AoC, affirmation of the consequent). Once the intervention effect (or lack of effect) is understood though a stable series of data, a third phase is initiated by removing the intervention. In this phase, the opportunity to verify the prediction is presented. Finally, the ideal design has a fourth phase to replicate the second phase and again observe the intervention effect. The result of this four-step process is the classic A-B-A-B design. This design is often referred to simply as a reversal design (Baer, Wolf, & Risley, 1968) or withdrawal design, as the model is attempting demonstrate the effect of an intervention by reversing the behavioral pattern or stopping academic progress. Although the A-B-A-B design is the classic method to document the relationship between an intervention and a target behavior, the subdesigns are also of unique importance in applied educational practice.

B Design

As discussed in Volume 1, Tier 1 interventions should be thoughtfully selected and outcome data on their effectiveness should be collected and analyzed. Although experimental design is not typically considered in Tier 1, the presentation of a stream of outcome data when a child is in a schoolwide intervention program (e.g., SWPBIS or a standard reading curriculum) documents their response to the Tier 1 intervention. Using the ABC coding system, this should be considered a one-phase B design.

Figure 4.5 is an example of a B design presented in an SCD graph. This example presents office discipline referral (ODR) data for a single class of students for the first 3 months

Intervention (B)

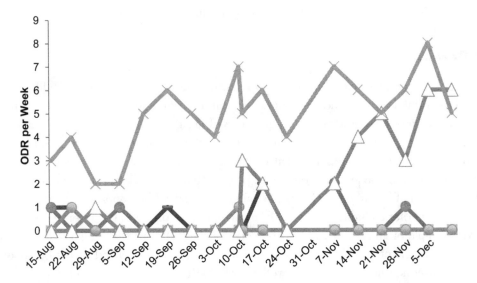

FIGURE 4.5. Example of a B design. Each student is presented in terms of number of weekly ODRs. A large number of students have no referrals and are clumped into the bottom square symbol.

of school. As can be seen in this example, most students have no violations resulting in an ODR and can be considered responsive to the classwide intervention. Three of the children have a few weeks in which an ODR was registered, but generally seem to be responding well to the classroom strategies. Although this design is not able to demonstrate a functional relationship between the classwide positive behavior supports and the student outcome data, this is not considered important at this stage of analysis. Simply put, the children are not behavioral concerns and would not be referred for additional consideration. Two children, though, seem to be displaying an interesting pattern of ODR. One child is exhibiting a consistent pattern of ODR, and clearly should be considered for Tier 2 support. The second child with an interesting pattern started the year with no documented issues, but has recently started to engage in behaviors resulting in an increasing rate of ODR. This child should also be considered for Tier 2 support.

This example displays the strengths and weakness of a B design. Starting with strengths, treating formative data collected to document the effectiveness of a schoolwide or classwide intervention (e.g., ODR, weekly spelling tests) as a B design allows educational professionals to use visual analysis to consider outliers who may need additional supports. Although teachers often think that they know the students in need, children who exhibit lower levels of behavioral or academic problems can go unnoticed when more serious cases are present. Graphing the data is a much more consistent method to identify all children in need. The primary weakness of B designs is the lack of potential to document experimental control. In terms of baseline logic, a B design lacks a prediction statement, verification, and replication. One can argue that examining a child against a standard or in comparison to other children's data paths is an example of affirmation of the consequent, but even that is stretching the logic. B designs should not be considered experimental, but rather a method to make identifying children in need of additional supports more consistent.

A-B Design

Once identified as needing additional supports, the next logical step in an RTI system is to develop an intervention and try it out. From an experimental standpoint this brings us to the second step in a withdrawal design, the A-B design. In an A-B design a stable series of baseline data is followed up by an intervention phase. The A-B design uses two of the steps of baseline logic, prediction and affirmation of the consequent, to answer the question "Did the outcome behavior change in close proximity to the initiation of the intervention?" As the core goal of any intervention is to change some target behavior, it is logically critical to measure whether a change occurred from the baseline phase to the intervention phase.

An example of an A-B design is provided in Figure 4.6. In this example, a child with high levels of disruptive behavior as documented by teacher-recorded direct behavior rating in the baseline phase (A) is monitored after an EBI is used (B). As can be seen, there is an immediate decrease in the amount of disruptive behavior recorded after the intervention was implemented. When graphed, this example shows how conveniently intervention progress can be demonstrated with an A-B presentation.

As with the B design, the strengths and weakness of this model are easily understood through a consideration of baseline logic. While an A-B design incorporates two phases of baseline logic—prediction and affirmation of the consequent—it is understood that without verification and replication this is only quasi-experimental. As such, an A-B design does not

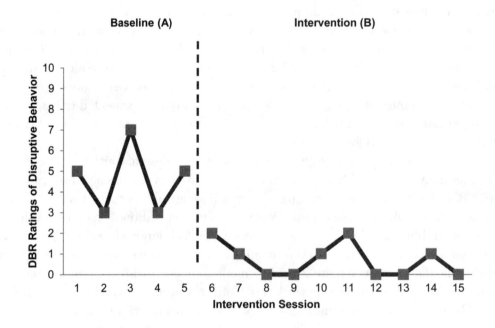

FIGURE 4.6. Example of an A-B design.

provide the opportunity to confidently suggest that any change observed is directly related to the intervention. Unfortunately, some other variable could be controlling the outcome data and truly be responsible for any observed change. While this is a significant weakness in the design, *if* documentation of a relationship between the intervention and the outcome data is not necessary then the model is highly useful. Specifically, an A-B design should be used in *any* intervention case were an EBI has been selected and implemented for a student in need. Consider for a minute the problem with an intervention case where an A-B design in not implemented. In such a case, the lack of defensible prediction statement followed by a demonstration of the outcome data when the intervention is present essentially removes any opportunity for educational professionals to suggest whether a change occurred. While the use of a functionally appropriate EBI increases the odds that a child will respond to an intervention, it is understood that this does not mean that the child will surely respond (see Volume 1 for an in-depth explanation of this issue). Specifically, only after a response has been demonstrated is there any true evidence that the intervention is evidence based for the specific case. Without the A-B design there is essentially no opportunity to make a statement about the effectiveness of the intervention. In an RTI model, this is simply unacceptable. In the end, the A-B design, in combination with the B design, should be the most frequently utilized design in an RTI system, as most decisions don't necessitate experimental control (Riley-Tillman & Burns, 2009).

> **An A-B design should be used in *any* intervention case where an EBI has been selected and implemented for a student in need.**

A-B-A Design

Although B and A-B designs are logically useful, an A-B-A design, the final subdesign of the full A-B-A-B, has particular importance in an RTI model. In this design, baseline data are collected, an intervention is implemented, and then the intervention is withdrawn (see Figure 4.7 for an example).

At face value, there seems to be little logic with this design. In the case of an intervention that seems to be effective there is no reason to remove the intervention and then not to return to the intervention condition (which would be an A-B-A-B design). In the case of an intervention that does not seem to be effective, it would seem somewhat irrelevant to "return to baseline," as the behavior in the intervention phase did not differ from the baseline phase. Unfortunately, this second case is not a safe assumption.

Figure 4.8 presents a case where it seems like the intervention is ineffective, but when it is withdrawn, the behavior drops to levels lower than observed in the baseline phase. If you remember the original discussion about the baseline phase, it was noted that the prediction statement was to be treated as tentative, and not fully trusted in the absence of verification. While we would like to assume that in the case of an incorrect prediction statement the error is in the direction of a child getting better, that will not always be the case. Figure 4.8 demonstrates how important returning to baseline actually is in an RTI model as a "nonresponse" is often treated as evidence for the need to accelerate the case. In that

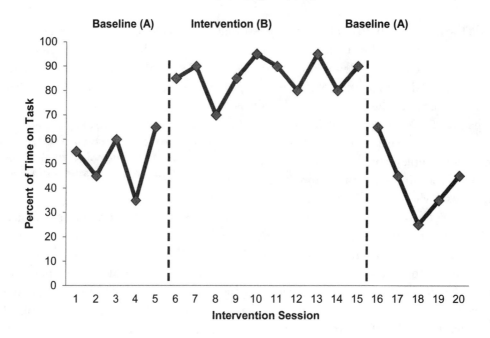

FIGURE 4.7. A-B-A design: Example 1.

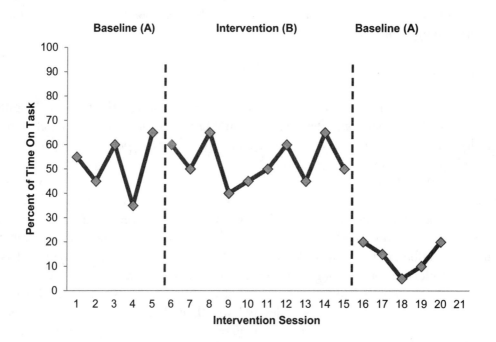

FIGURE 4.8. A-B-A design: Example 2.

example, though, what would have appeared to be a nonresponse actually seems to be a partial response, as the intervention was sustaining baseline level. There is also a secondary benefit of returning to baseline. Logically, a different intervention will be attempted, and the return to baseline allows a period of time to pass so that back-to-back interventions are not applied. If that precaution is not taken, then any analysis of the new intervention (C) should consider that the B phase intervention may have had a priming effect on the intervention in the C phase.

A-B-A-B Design

As noted above, the A-B-A-B design is the one of the classic SCDs that has the full potential to demonstrate experimental control. Using baseline logic to describe the design, the initial A phase is the prediction statement suggesting what would occur in the future if no intervention was attempted. In the initial B phase the intervention is implemented and any effect is observed. After a steady stream of data is observed, the intervention is discontinued in the second B phase in order to verify the predication statement. Finally, the intervention is replicated in the final A phase to again observe the intervention effect. As the goal of an A-B-A-B design is to demonstrate a functional relationship between the intervention and the target behavior, it is important to consider what the data pattern should look like for there to be evidence of experimental control. Figure 4.9 demonstrates an A-B-A-B design with evidence of experimental control. In this example, a stable baseline (A) is demonstrated followed by the application of the intervention. In this case, there is an immediate intervention effect that is critical in order to attribute the change to the intervention. The B phase is continued until the outcome data are stable, and then the intervention is removed to begin the withdrawal phase (A). In this phase, it is expected that the data either return to baseline

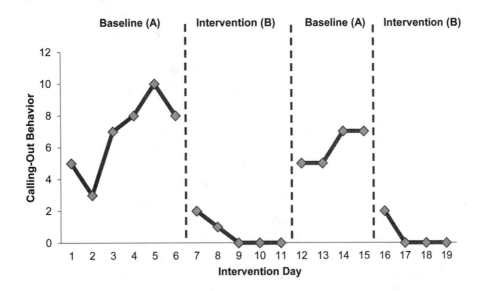

FIGURE 4.9. Example of an A-B-A-B design.

levels (for interventions where there is no learned behavior) or to baseline trends (for interventions where there is a learned behavior). In this case, once the return to baseline was stable, the intervention was again implemented and the outcome data again demonstrated an effect. In this example, this point is where the argument can be mounted that the intervention was responsible for the observed change in outcome data.

Multiple-Baseline Design

While withdrawal designs have some significant strengths, they also have one major weakness—the mandated removal of the intervention. A popular SCD called the multiple-baseline (MB) design accomplishes verification and replication by conducting the intervention in a number of "conditions" with different start date. As a result, there is no need for an intervention to be removed. Specifically, MB designs are created by using several A-B designs, all of which have the same intervention and target behavior but a staggered implementation of the treatment. The term *condition* is very important to define before proceeding. MB designs are typically composed of "subjects" (e.g., three subjects who get the same intervention at different times), settings (e.g., intervention is conducted with the same child in three settings at different times), or stimuli (e.g., the intervention is conducted with the same child but with a different set of stimuli at different times). Each of these versions results in a different type of MB, which can be used for different purposes. We outline the varieties of MB later in this section.

The most critical feature of the MB design is the use of a "lag" in implementing the intervention. Essentially, in the first condition the intervention is implemented when there is a sufficient baseline while concurrently in the other conditions, baseline data continue to be collected in the absence of intervention. The goal is to observe a response to intervention in the condition where the intervention is implemented and no alteration in the target behavior in the other conditions (see Figure 4.10). In this situation, conditions 2 and 3 provide verification that without intervention the predicted target behavior in baseline would continue. Replication is accomplished by repeating this process for all remaining conditions. If we observe changes only when the intervention is implemented there is support that a functional relationship exists between the intervention and the target behavior. If, on the other hand, we observe changes in the absence of intervention (e.g., a change in on-task behavior in conditions 2 and 3 when the intervention is applied only in condition 1), then there is a clear concern that some unknown variables are controlling the target behavior.

When selecting the condition, it is important to think about the different subjects, settings, or stimuli included. Ideally, they will be as similar as possible without a risk of contamination. The need for conditions to be similar is rather obvious. There is little reason to think very different children will respond to the same intervention. Likewise, a child is not likely to respond to the same intervention in dissimilar settings. By selecting similar conditions, they should respond to the intervention in a parallel manner, assuming the intervention is functionally related to the target behavior. Another advantage of selecting similar conditions is that many external variables should affect them in the same manner. The second issue—"without risk of contamination"—is less intuitive. Because an MB design

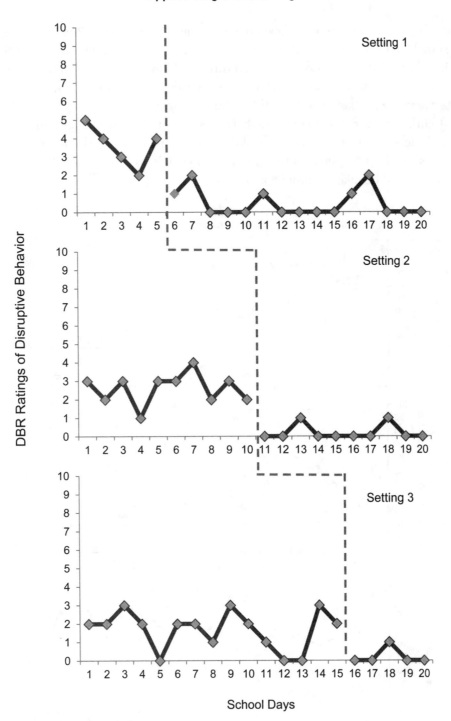

FIGURE 4.10. Multiple-baseline across-setting example.

relies on the intervention being delayed in conditions 2, 3, etc., when it is in place in condition 1, any bleed-over effect of the intervention from condition 1 to other conditions can result in a destroyed design. For example, if three children are selected in the same class to test a teacher-run intervention, and the teacher decides on his or her own to start parts of the intervention with the second and third children right after seeing a positive effect with the first child, the design is undermined. This contamination can happen in a number of manners (teachers talking to each other, skills learned on one setting being tried out by the child in a second setting, etc.) and is virtually impossible to fully avoid. Regardless, some precaution should be taken to avoid contamination.

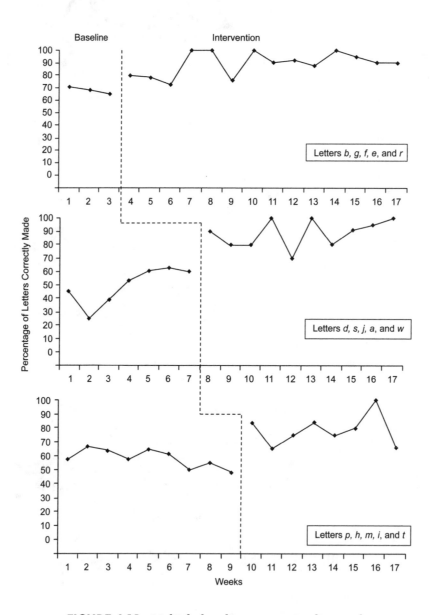

FIGURE 4.11. Multiple-baseline across-stimuli example.

As discussed above, the type of condition selected influences what is learned from the design. An MB design across subjects design is used to document that the intervention has a generalizable effect. In that design, when successful, it is documented that the intervention works across a number of similar children. MBs across setting or stimuli designs are used to observe the consistency of the intervention effect with one child. In the case of MB across setting, a successful design can show an intervention effect in a variety of settings. MB across stimuli is ideal for determining a functional relationship between an intervention and target behavior in a single setting.

Figure 4.11 provides a good example using the case of a child who is exhibiting severe penmanship difficulties. To evaluate the effect of an EBI, an MB design was used with three conditions composed of different "letter groups." Due to the nature of the intervention, there was no concern that the intervention would bleed over to nontarget letters. The intervention was first used with condition 1 (letters *b*, *g*, *f*, *e*, and *r*), and an immediate change in level and trend was observed while conditions 2 and 3 did not show improvement. The intervention was then implemented with condition 2 followed by condition 3, with similar effects. This MB example shows clear support that the intervention is responsible for the improvement in penmanship. Although MB designs take a deeper understanding of baseline logic to use in practice, they are very helpful in cases where a withdrawal is not possible, or simply not ethical.

THE ROLE OF SINGLE-CASE DESIGN IN A RESPONSE-TO-INTERVENTION MODEL

As noted several times throughout this book, the heart of an RTI model is the question of whether a child responded to EBI. While this question is important throughout Tiers 1, 2 and 3, the specific nature of the question is quite different. Starting with Tier 1, it is not important to actually link an observed response to a specific intervention. Considering the number of cases, attempting to use experimental methods with a large number of Tier 1 cases will tax the resources of schools and would arguably be unethical because there is no reason to delay service if a child is continuously responding. In contrast, in Tier 3 when eligibility for services is linked to a belief that an observed response is directly related to intervention or package of interventions, it is important to be able to link a child's response to a particular EBI. SCD provides the technology to document a child's response to intervention at both nonexperimental and fully experimental levels. As a general guideline, we suggest the following.

The primary application of SCD in Tier 1 is the use of B designs in a manner analogous to a car's dashboard. If all is well, the gauges reflect appropriate figures and can essentially be ignored. In the case of a problem, the check-engine light illumines and the driver knows further action should be taken. Likewise, when a child starts to perform in a manner outside of the typical range, it is understood that he or she should receive more attention. This use of the dashboard, or B designs in schools, creates a quick detection system to prompt intervention to avoid serious damage. In some Tier 1 cases it will be important to document that a target behavior changed after a unique intervention was applied. An A-B design is ideal for this situation: it is not critical to demonstrate a functional relationship, yet a clear statement about "change" or "lack of change" can be provided. At this stage, a feasible attempt to use SCD is sufficient.

In Tier 2 we shift the focus to cases where at the minimum it is important to document that change has or has not occurred after an intervention is started. To accomplish this goal SCD in Tier 2 should primarily be highly feasible nonexperimental designs (e.g. B and A-B) with fully experimental approaches (A-B-A-B and MB) considered only in selected cases where such an approach may prove useful. Another general goal of Tier 2 is to start to consider function with intervention selection. While full use of functional assessment strategies is typically beyond the scope of Tier 2, SCD can be used to start testing hypotheses generated about academic and behavior cases. At this stage we again suggest that feasibility be strongly considered when selecting a design so that GLTs or PSTs are not overly taxed with complex designs.

> While full use of functional assessment strategies is typically beyond the scope of Tier 2, SCD can be used to start testing hypotheses generated about academic and behavior cases.

Gansle and Noell (2007) provided an enlightening comparison of making decisions using an RTI model without evidence that the model is being implemented correctly when they compared it to an evaluation team making decisions without conducting an evaluation. This example can be logically extended to the case where decisions are made about a child's "response to an intervention" in the absence of data that an observed change was actually due to the intervention. In Tier 3 the issues of eligibility may be addressed, and predictably we suggest that fully experimental designs be the backbone of SCD use at this stage. To confidently state that a child should be classified as LD due to their response to a specific intervention, we must be able to document that there is a functional relationship between the intervention and the target behaviors. It is critical to note that SCD is in this case being used to identify interventions that work, and then consider whether continuing those interventions requires the support of special education. When used in conjunction with EBI, assessment, and decision making, SCD is an ideal technology to clearly identify interventions that work across each tier of service.

CONCLUSION

RTI at its core is a model developed to allow a more experimental approach to serve children's educational needs. While the intensity of evidence-based practice varies across the tiers, SCD provides the ideal technology for schools to evaluate RTI. Unfortunately, there is not significant use of even the most basic elements of SCD in schools today. While B and A-B designs at a minimum should be in place nationwide, in our experience their use is the exception to standard practice. Obviously, advanced SCD has very little history in most schools.

Our suggestion for educational professionals interested in incorporating SCD into their schools is to start very slowly. Simply using B and A-B designs would be a significant advancement for most schools. It may take years for schools to consistently collect pre–post data on children and evaluate the effect of EBIs. Despite the challenge, this process should have a great deal of benefit for all children. In relation to advanced SCD, while the ability to demonstrate experimental control can be very useful, there is no need to be dogmatic. Rather, schools should simply build up technical expertise and use such methods when useful and necessary. The first cases where the application of advanced SCD is likely to be necessary are with severe behavior cases where identification of function is essential. In time, the benefits of using of nonreversal designs (e.g., MB designs) for severe academic cases will become apparent as school staff members gain experience and comfort using SCD.

Often the timelines for the evaluation are such that an effective intervention cannot be identified at the time of eligibility determination. When timelines force a decision prior to identification of effective intervention, we suggest that systems be put in place to ensure that teams will continue to work toward finding effective EBI through the individualized education program (IEP) process. Specifically, one model that has been successful is to set up a system of review where IEPs are randomly reviewed and evaluated for quality indicators (e.g., graphs with phase change lines, objective data in present levels of educational performance [PLEP], measurable goals and objectives) and then report these results by teacher, building, and district using a rubric to assign numerical value to each area. Whereas ideally effective intervention is a known when a child is determined eligible for special education services, other methods can promote the continued use of SCD to identify effective services.

Regardless of the stage of SCD use, the goal is to keep the focus on finding interventions that work rather than labeling a child and becoming comfortable that "special education" will solve the problems. SCD at any level can help educational professionals evaluate whether the interventions they are using are working. This true understanding of RTI is a critical issue for all children, especially children in need.

CHAPTER 5

Evaluating Interventions
Analysis of Intervention Data

When working in the field we are often struck by the dramatic progress that has been made over the last decade. Schools have embraced EBI at the whole-school, classwide, small-group, and individual level, and the amount of data collected by teachers is simply amazing. Schools are long past the stage where formative assessment was a concept of the future. Unfortunately, there seems to have been less focus on training educational professionals to make decisions with data. All the data in the world are worthless unless they are analyzed correctly and services are altered appropriately. In the data analysis phase, educational professionals can finally answer three critical questions:

1. How much of a change was there in the target behavior?
2. Was any observed change the result of the attempted intervention?
3. Does any documented change place the child on a path to a successful outcome?

In this we chapter we review the most defensible methods to analyze intervention data. Please note, all examples in this chapter use simulated data.

SUMMARIZING DATA THROUGH VISUAL PRESENTATION: CREATING THE LINE GRAPH

In our experience the most effective manner in which to display intervention data is a simple line graph. Intervention data by definition are collected over time. Line graphs were developed to document how a target behavior changed from start to finish. Consider for a minute the amount of information provided in Figure 5.1. In one quick look, we know the target behavior (calling out), the range of the behavior prior to intervention (8–14 times a

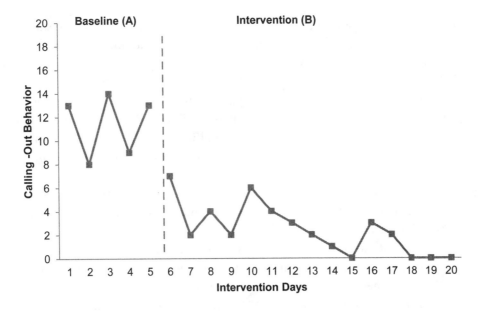

FIGURE 5.1. Sample intervention graph.

day), the range of the behavior after the intervention began (0–7), the trend of the behavior, the length of the intervention, and so on. While the graph does not tell the whole story, it provides much of the critical information in a convenient package. To make the most of this approach, we suggest that schools use one consistent method of graphing intervention data so educational professionals become accustomed to a particular presentation.

> **We suggest that schools use one consistent method of graphing intervention data so educational professionals become accustomed to a particular presentation.**

Single-Case-Design Graphing Guidelines

While there is no single reference to guide the creation of intervention graphs, there is a loose set of guidelines that are widely adopted by those who utilize SCD. Once understood, these conventions make it rather easy for a reader to understand what is being represented in an SCD graph. We believe that in applied educational settings, consistent presentation of intervention graphs will greatly assist educational professionals when they learn how to analyze intervention data. When a teacher, team, and school each use their own methods, it takes time for consumers to fully understand the grant. In contrast, a standard graphing protocol will minimize confusion and assist discussion about the child and intervention rather than explanation of the data presentation. In this section, we outline the model presented in Riley-Tillman and Burns (2009) that combined suggestions from a variety of sources including Tawney and Gast (1984), and Cooper and colleagues (2007). The basic standards for an SCD graph are as follows (from Riley-Tillman & Burns, 2009):

1. Each target behavior should have its own series of data which use the same marker (e.g., ■, O, or ▲). Tawney and Gast (1984) suggest that no more than three target behaviors be plotted on any single graph. It is our experience that every additional behavior on a graph makes interpretation more difficult. As such, in an educational environment where consumers will typically have limited experience (at least initially) with such data presentations, it is advisable to graph outcome behaviors on separate graphs unless there is a compelling reason to combine them into one presentation (e.g., graphing related behaviors like words correct per minute and errors).

2. Each series of data should have a line that connects data points. This process creates what is called a *data path*. There are several important conventions regarding data paths (Cooper et al., 2007).
   a. Data points should only be connected within a phase.
   b. If a significant amount of time has passed (see 5c below), the data points before and after the break should not be connected.
   c. If planned data are not available for any reason, the data points before and after the unavailable data should not be connected.
   d. Follow-up data (any data collected at a later date to check on the target behavior) that are not collected in the same interval as the initial data (e.g., A-B-A-B data were collected daily for 4 weeks and follow-up data were collected bimonthly for 2 months following the end of the initial design) should not be connected with each other.

3. Phase changes should be noted on a line graph with a vertical line. The vertical line can be solid or dashed. We suggest using a dashed line, as it draws attention to the phase change and looks different than a data path.

4. The *y*-axis (vertical axis) should be used to represent the outcome data.
   a. The scale should be appropriate for the target behavior and use an equal interval.
   b. It is important to present the minimum and maximum values possible in the scale for the *y*-axis (e.g., 0% on task to 100% on task). If the outcome data are not evenly distributed (e.g., ranging from 5 to 25%) it is acceptable to scale the graph partially (e.g., 0–50%), then place a scale break (//) in the *y*-axis above the highest number in the selected scale (50% in this case) and then extend the scale to 100% immediately above the scale break.

5. The *x*-axis (horizontal axis) should be used to represent time.
   a. The earliest recording of the outcome data should be placed next to the *y*-axis, and the most recent on the far right of the *x*-axis with an equal interval in between.
   b. The units should be a logical representation of the case. Thus for a whole-day intervention, "intervention day" could be used. If multiple intervention sessions occurred each day, it would be more appropriate to use "intervention session."
   c. If there is a gap in time (e.g., winter break), the *x*-axis should have a // placed

on the line between the last point before the break and the first point after the break. This informs the reader that there was an interruption in the phase.

6. Labels for both the *x*- and *y*-axes should be utilized, and should briefly orient the reader to that axis.

7. Tawney and Gast (1984) suggest that the ideal ratio of the *y*-axis to the *x*-axis is 2:3. They contend that this presentation minimizes visual distortion that can occur with a longer *y*-axis (e.g., 3:3 ratio) or longer *x*-axis (e.g., 2:4 ratio).

Building Intervention Graphs

Using these standards, it is simple to create A-B, A-B-A-B, and MB graphs. You can use Forms 5.1–5.3 at the end of this chapter when graphing by hand. For those more technically proficient, these steps can be applied using software packages like Microsoft Excel to develop professional-looking graphs.

Steps for Developing a Simple A-B Intervention Graph (from Riley-Tillman & Burns, 2009)

1. Label the *y* (vertical) axis with behavior of interest (e.g., words correct per minute).

2. Select the scale for the *y*-axis based on the data collected (e.g., 0 to 100% for percentage of time on task or percentage of intervals of out of seat or number of words correct per minute).

3. Select the scale for and label the *x* (horizontal) axis with observation intervals (e.g., day, period, week).

4. Separate preintervention (baseline) and intervention phase data with a vertical dashed line (e.g., 5 days of baseline data followed by 15 days of intervention).

5. Connect consecutive data points within phases to show progress. To summarize data within phases, do not connect lines across phases (i.e., preintervention to intervention).

6. Repeat steps as needed to develop A-B-A and A-B-A-B design graphs.

Steps for Developing a Multiple-Baseline Intervention Graph (from Riley-Tillman & Burns, 2009) (see Figure 5.2 for an example):

1. Replicate the steps for an A-B graph for the first, second, and third target (e.g., behaviors, subjects, setting, or other).

2. Place the A-B graph where the intervention will be implemented first at the top of the page.

3. Place the next A-B graph representing the second intervention implemented under the first.

4. Place the final A-B graph under the second. Repeat for all successive targets.

5. Connect the three intervention phases with a stair-step line to document the shifting implementation of the intervention.

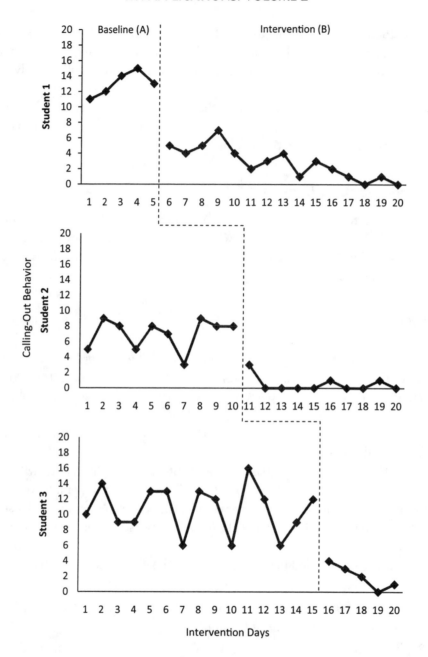

FIGURE 5.2. Sample multiple-baseline graph. From Riley-Tillman and Burns (2009). Copyright 2009 by The Guilford Press. Reprinted by permission.

ANALYSIS OF AN INTERVENTION EFFECT: "WAS THERE A CHANGE?"

Once data have been graphed, we can answer the quintessential question of an RTI model: "Did the child respond to the intervention?" To increase clarity, we break that question into two subquestions, each of which requires a different analytic plan (Horner et al., 2005):

1. "To what degree was there a change in the target behavior(s) when the intervention was implemented (or removed)?"
2. "Can we say that the intervention was responsible for the observed change?"

Question 1 addresses the issue of "change" or, conversely, "lack of change." Otherwise stated, this path focuses on whether the child's behavior is now on a more desirable pathway. Analysis regarding this question focuses on amount of change, the trend of the change, and the type of change. All of this information is critical when considering whether, after the intervention, the child is now on a path to a successful outcome, or whether changes to the intervention are necessary. Question 2 gets to a more detailed issue, specifically, whether we can defensibly link the observed change to the intervention. In some cases, this question can't be asked, as many SCDs don't have the potential for demonstrating a functional relationship (e.g., A, A-B and A-B-A). In other situations, when a design can document a functional relationship (e.g., A-B-A-B or MB), it is critical to assess whether the data performed in a manner so that a full demonstration of baseline logic occurred. Before addressing Question 2, we will start with an overview of how to use visual analysis to establish whether there is a change after an intervention has been implemented.

"To What Degree Was There a Change in the Target Behavior(s) When the Intervention Was Implemented (or Removed)?"

When documenting an intervention effect or lack of effect, we suggest starting with visual analysis. Unlike some of the more recent methods of analysis, which we discuss below, visual analysis has an extensive history in education, school psychology, applied behavior analysis, and many other disciplines. This history has resulted in an extensive vetting of visual analysis as a defensible analytic method. The primary components of visual analysis we focus on are examining (1) level, (2) trend, (3) variability, and (4) immediacy. Before diving into each area, it is important to first note that, depending on the situation, each method may have more or less importance. For example, when examining the effect of a reading intervention it is likely that trend will be of utmost importance with some focus on level changes. On the other hand, interventions focusing on minimizing disruptive behavioral typically focus on variability, immediacy, and level. As we review each method, consider in which situations they would prove useful, or those in which they are not an appropriate analysis strategy. Before moving on, it is important to note that we orient the following section to focus on documenting "change." In an RTI model it is also important to document a "lack of change." It is appropriate to argue that the absence of observed changes in level, trend, variability, and/or immediacy suggests that there is no evidence for a response to intervention. The lack of evidence for response to intervention can be used to build a case for a target student's nonresponse.

Change in Level

In most cases, problem behavior is described as not enough or too much of something. For example, reading problems are often due to low levels of accuracy and a high number of errors. In the case of a behavior problem it is typical to hear about too much disruptive behavior with not enough academic engagement. In any of these cases one of the main goals is to raise the level of something desired, and lower the level of something problematic. As such, one of the most basic ways in which to consider SCD outcome data is to look at the mean or median in the baseline phase and compare that to the mean or median in the intervention phase. Going back to Figure 5.1, the mean number of observed calling-out behavior after intervention (2.4) was considerably less than in the baseline phase (11.4). Another way to consider the same data is to consider the median level in each phase (baseline phase: 13, intervention phase: 2). While in this example there is not utility of using the median, in many cases it is the much more defensible statistic. Consider the current example. If the child had very bad days in the middle of the intervention phase and registered 13 and 14 on days 13 and 14, the mean in the intervention phase would shift from 2.4 up to 4. Those days may be considered outliers and an explanation exists as to why they are not representative of behavior in the intervention phase. In that case the median of the intervention phase would have shifted to 3, the more appropriate descriptive statistic. In SCD, where outliers can be particularly significant due to the typicality of small data sets, the role of outliers should be considered. This example also cautions about only using one method of visual analysis. Although focusing on level change did demonstrate that the behavior altered in the intervention phase, it misses that in the intervention phase there is a decreasing trend that results in essentially no disruptive behavior in the final days (0, 1, and 0 instances of disruptive behavior).

Change in Trend

Considering that many interventions in schools focus on academic behavior, examining changes in the rate of learning is quite important. Starting with the basics, a stream of outcome data is generally increasing, decreasing, or stable within a phase (the issue of variable data is addressed later in this chapter). The trend of the data is documenting the rate at which a behavior changes over a period of time. In most academic interventions the trend of the target behavior is stable or slowly increasing in the baseline phase. The goal of intervention in that case is not to document a full level change, but rather to document the rate at which the target behavior is increasing. For example, if in baseline a child is increasing words read correctly in 1 minute by 0.5 words each week, the child is not likely on a pathway to reach desired benchmarks. In such a case, increasing the rate to three words per week suggests that the child is making six times the progress. That trend can then be used to see whether over X amount of time the child will reach some desired level of reading.

Considering trends is also important in examining whether a "difference" exists between phases. If in the baseline there is a decreasing trend of calling-out statements, that suggests the child is moving in the right direction in the absence of the intervention. Even if an intervention effect is observed, one can't say whether it was the intervention or simply the extension of what was observed in the baseline phase.

To consider the impact of baseline trend on the intervention phase, see Figure 5.3. In this figure, three intervention graphs are presented that have the same intervention data presented in each case, but different "types" of baselines. In the first case, an ascending trend in the baseline phase is observed that, when used as a prediction statement, suggests that the intervention data would likely have been observed in the absence of intervention. This case would not be considered documentation of an intervention effect, as no change from the prediction statement is observed. In the second case, a level trend is observed in the baseline phase that predicts that, without intervention, words correct per minute would continue in the 5–7 range. Because the behavior in the intervention phase was observed in the 11–18 range with an ascending trend, this case would be seen as a documentation of an intervention effect. In the final case, a descending baseline is observed, which suggests the child's reading is actually deteriorating over time. When followed with the behavior observed in the intervention phase in the 11–18 range with an ascending trend, this is an example of an even more robust intervention effect, as not only the level changed, but the trend was reversed. In summary, these three cases help demonstrate how trends in baseline should be considered in relation to considering an intervention effect.

Change in Variability

While increasing or decreasing the level or trend is typically the goal of intervention, in some cases the goal is simply to remove variability. Variability refers to the range in a set of data. Particularly in the case of behavior intervention, children display a full range of behavior (e.g., on task 90% one observation but 15% the next). For example, even in the case of a student who is described as highly disengaged yet has the skill to be engaged, if you observe the child for long enough she will demonstrate several instances of "engaged" behavior. As discussed extensively in Volume 1, in cases where the goal is to increase the proficiency of appropriate behavior, the expectation is simply to increase the rate of the desired interaction. In such cases, the analytic focus should include the variability of the target behavior with the goal of minimizing the variability of the target behavior rather than to demonstrate some altogether new level.

In Figure 5.4, data are presented from a classwide intervention targeted at decreasing students' "out-of-seat" behavior. Not surprisingly, in the baseline phase there is a great deal of variability. In some sessions there is very little out-of-seat behavior; in others, very high rates. In this case, the mean of the out-of-seat behavior would not be an ideal estimate of out-of-seat behavior.

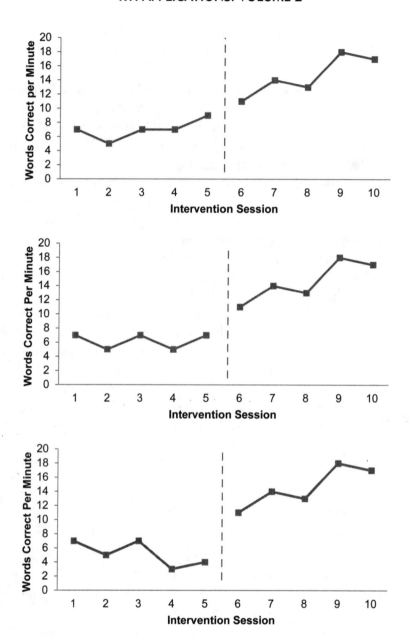

FIGURE 5.3. Sample intervention graph: Impact of baseline-phase trends on the intervention phase.

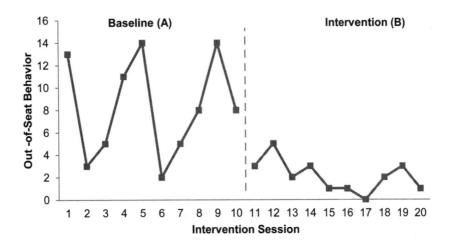

FIGURE 5.4. Sample intervention graph: Decreased variability.

There are several ways to discuss the variably observed. First, a high–low range can be used as a simple method to express variability of data within the phase. In Figure 5.4, out-of-seat behavior ranged from 2 to 16 in the baseline phase. In contrast, after an intervention was attempted the range of out of seat behavior decreased to a 0–5 range. Another method to capture variability is to present the number of nonoverlapping data points. In the current case, 60% of the data in baseline do not overlap with data in the intervention phase.

It is important for a minute to consider that decreasing variability is functionally the same thing as changing the level or trend where there is no overlap between phases. If there is a full level shift with no overlap, then the behavior observed in the intervention phase is at a fully new level. In the case of decreased variability in an intervention phase with overlap with the baseline phase, the behavior is not considered "different" as it has been observed. For example, in Figure 5.4, the students in the class had demonstrated appropriate behavior in the baseline. Postintervention, the students in the class have not demonstrated a new behavior, but rather have started more consistently to demonstrate the appropriate behavior.

One final consideration in terms of variably of data is to ensure that sufficient data are collected within a phase so that an accurate assessment of variance can be made. With stable data (e.g., 10%, 10%, 15%, 10%) a summary statement can be made after only a few data points. In the case of highly variable data such as in Figure 5.4, though, it is critical to collect enough data to fully capture the pattern of variability. If, for example, data vacillate from variable to consistent, then data collection must continue in that phase until a defensible summary statement can be developed.

Immediacy/Latency of Change

One of the most important categories of visual analysis is examining how quickly behavior change occurs after the intervention is started. The "immediacy" of the intervention will become critical later, when we consider whether the intervention caused a change in the

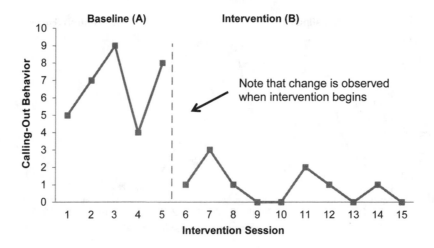

FIGURE 5.5. Sample intervention graph: Immediacy of change.

target behavior. Ideally, there is a large predicted increase or decrease in the target behavior in the first observation after the intervention started (see Figure 5.5 for an example). Logically, there will be some interventions in which this is not expected, but even with interventions that are intended to result in a gradual increase in trend, that trend change preferably occurs in the first three to five observations after the intervention starts.

The opposite of an immediate intervention impact is a latent one. In some cases there will be a reason to believe that an intervention will result in changes after *X* amount of time. For example, in the case of a multistage social behavior training intervention with children who have social skills deficits, one might postulate that at the end of the third training session a specific skill will be learned and a change in target behavior will be likely. In that

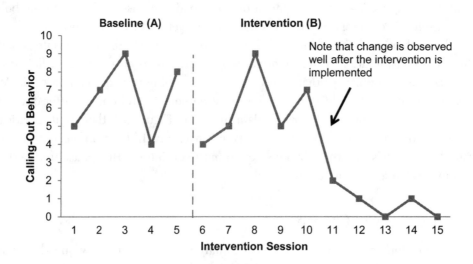

FIGURE 5.6. Sample intervention graph: Latency of change.

case, a latent response would be predicted and acceptable. In the absence of an a priori reason for a latent response, a delayed response is concerning. As such, Figure 5.6 can be viewed in two ways. If it was understood before the intervention was initiated that there would be a delayed response, then a five-session delay in the behavior change is acceptable. If there was no reason to suggest the intervention would take time to change the child's behavior, then it seems likely something changed after five sessions, which resulted in the observed decrease in calling-out behavior. Unless we know what that change is, analysis of the intervention effect is difficult. Significant level or trend changes in the middle of a phase should be considered a threat to internal validity.

Considering the Interaction of Level, Variability, and Trend

Before ending the review of basic visual analysis, some discussion about interaction effects is important (Horner, 2008). Throughout the presentation of level, trend, variability, and immediacy/latency we have discussed the relationship of each category. For example, the amount of level or trend change affects our statement of immediacy. We also discussed the impact of trend in the baseline phase on the analysis of the intervention effect. Looking back to Figure 5.2, in that case the ascending trend in the first example predicted the behavior in the intervention phase. If in that case we were to simply look at level, the baseline mean of words correct per minute (WCPM) of 7 and the intervention phase mean of 14.6 would suggest that there was a large change in target behavior. Ignoring the trend when interpreting the level results in the incorrect conclusion that the path of the data changed. Likewise, in the third example in Figure 5.2, level analysis does not fully capture the reversal of the trend. Across cases variability, level, and trend can affect each other to enhance or mitigate what a single visual analysis focus might suggest. As such, it is critical to consider the case at hand and use all relevant methods of visual analysis to create as accurate an understanding of the target behavior as possible.

ANALYSIS OF A FUNCTIONAL RELATIONSHIP: "CAN WE SAY THAT THE INTERVENTION WAS RESPONSIBLE FOR THE OBSERVED CHANGE?"

Once it has been determined whether there has been a change, and what the nature of the change is, a second question can be considered: "Was the intervention the reason for the observed change?" The utility of this question in an RTI model has been discussed in several places in this book. Essentially, as the stakes of a particular case increase, the importance of documenting a functional relationship between an intervention and an outcome increases. If the decision is made to label a child LD due in part to a documented response to a highly intensive intervention, it is essential that the documented

> **As the stakes of a particular case increase, the importance of documenting a functional relationship between an intervention and an outcome increases.**

response was actually caused by the intensive intervention and not by some other variable or set of variables.

In Chapter 4 baseline logic was outlined as the pathway to documenting the relationship between an intervention and an outcome variable. Specifically, to be able to confidently state that an intervention "worked," each phase of baseline logic (prediction, affirmation of the consequent, verification, and replication) must be present. In the case of A-B-A-B and MB designs each of these phases is possible, but the pattern of data must follow the correct pattern before the intervention–outcome relationship can be claimed. What follows is a brief review of how the data should "dance" in SCD for educational professionals to be confident that the intervention is responsible for the change in behavior.

A-B-A-B Design

A-B-A-B designs have been created so that after a stable baseline is established, three separation demonstrations of the intervention effect can be observed.

1. (**A-B**-A-B)—In the first demonstration of the intervention effect, we see whether the intervention results in the predicted change in behavior. Typically, this would be an increase in a desired outcome (e.g., reading fluency or academic engagement) or decrease in an undesirable behavior (e.g., disruption).
2. (A-**B-A**-B)—In the second demonstration of the intervention effect, we see whether removing the intervention resulted in the predicted changed in the behavior. This would be the case if we see the desired increase or decrease observed in Step 1 reversed (typical with "behavior variables" like engagement) or slowed (typical with "academic" outcomes such as reading fluency).
3. (A-B-**A-B**)—In the final demonstration of the intervention effect, we see whether the reintroduction of the intervention results in the predicted behavior change. This is simply the replication of Step 1.

This approach is consistent with that suggested by Horner and colleagues (2005). Specifically, they argue that it takes three demonstrations of a predicted change in outcome data when the intervention is introduced or removed to document experimental control. Horner and his colleagues use the term *experimental effects*. Experimental effects are any predicted changes in outcome data that occur concurrently with manipulations of the intervention.

As an example, see Figure 5.7, where an A-B-A-B design was utilized to understand the relationship between the intervention and the target behavior (on-task behavior). In this case, each stage of baseline logic is defensibly presented.

- *Prediction.* There is a stable baseline with a slightly descending trend.
- *Affirmation of the Consequent.* When the intervention is applied, there is an immediate change in the level of on-task behavior. The slightly descending trend present in the baseline phase reverses to an ascending pattern.

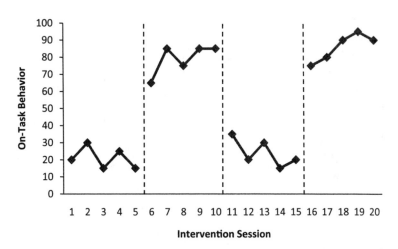

FIGURE 5.7. A-B-A-B graph supporting experimental control. From Riley-Tillman and Burns (2009). Copyright 2009 by The Guilford Press. Reprinted by permission.

- *Verification.* When the intervention is removed, there is an immediate drop in level, and the trend reverts to the same descending pattern observed in the baseline phase.
- *Replication.* When the intervention is reintroduced, the first affirmation of the consequent is replicated with an immediate change in level and trend in the predicted direction.

In this case, visual analysis not only supports that there was a change, but that there is support for a full expression of baseline logic. Using Horner and colleagues' (2005) approach, there were three clearly demonstrated experimental effects. This combination supports that there was a "response to the specific intervention."

Figure 5.8 presents a second A-B-A-B design. In this case, visual analysis does not support the argument that the intervention is clearly the reason for any observed change. Specifically, when the intervention was removed the prediction statement was not verified. Rather, academic engagement remained at intervention levels in the absence of the intervention. As such, there is significant risk that some other unknown variable is responsible for the observed change in academic engagement. Using Horner and colleagues' (2005) model, visual analysis supports only one experimental effect. There are clearly two ways to consider these data. The glass-half-full approach focuses on the demonstration of behavior change. The glass-half-empty approach realizes that no one can state with confidence what caused that change.

Multiple-Baseline Design

As discussed in Chapter 4, MB designs can provide evidence that an intervention is responsible for an observed change in outcome data, assuming each stage of baseline logic is demonstrated. As an example, see Figure 5.9, where an MB design was utilized to understand

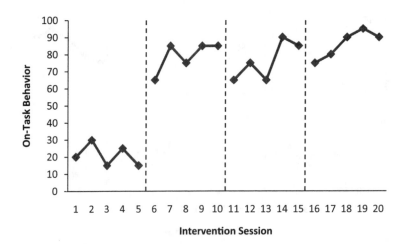

FIGURE 5.8. A-B-A-B graph without support for experimental control. From Riley-Tillman and Burns (2009). Copyright 2009 by The Guilford Press. Reprinted by permission.

the relationship between the intervention and the target behavior. In this case, each stage of baseline logic is defensibly presented.

- *Prediction.* There is a stable baseline in the first setting with a slightly descending trend.
- *Affirmation of the Consequent.* When the intervention is applied, there is an immediate change in the level of on-task behavior. The slightly descending trend present in the baseline phase reverts to a stable pattern.
- *Verification.* In settings 2 and 3 there is no alteration in baseline data when the intervention is implemented in setting 1. This suggests there is no variable external to the three settings controlling the behavior in setting 1.
- *Replication.* When the intervention is introduced in setting 2, the first affirmation of the consequent (in setting 1) is replicated with an immediate change in level and trend in the predicted direction. This then replicated again in setting 3.

Figure 5.9 is an excellent example of an MB design where a full expression of baseline logic supports that the intervention is responsible for the observed change in the target behavior. Using Horner and colleagues' (2005) approach there are three clear demonstrations of an experimental effect. Specifically, in an MB design each linked A-B provides one opportunity to observe an experimental effect. In Figure 5.10, alterations in the baseline data for settings 2 and 3 draw into question the relationship between the intervention and the outcome data. In this example, there appears to be a change in settings 2 and 3 when there is no intervention in place. This results in the lack of verification of the prediction statement, and does not allow one to conclude the response is functionally related to the intervention. This case also provides only one demonstration of an experimental effect. Of course, the child does seem to be improving, which is excellent news mitigated only by

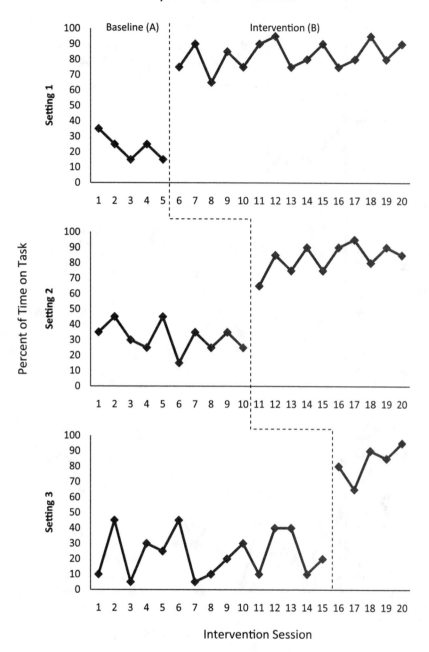

FIGURE 5.9. Multiple baseline supporting experimental control. From Riley-Tillman and Burns (2009). Copyright 2009 by The Guilford Press. Reprinted by permission.

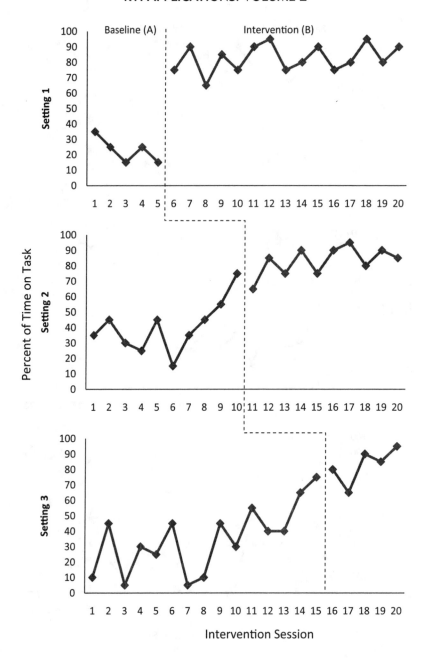

FIGURE 5.10. Multiple baseline without support for experimental control. From Riley-Tillman and Burns (2009). Copyright 2009 by The Guilford Press. Reprinted by permission.

a lack of evidence as to why the change occurred. The type of decision being made will determine the importance of the lack of experimental control. In a low-stakes case the change in on-task behavior could simply be monitored. If the child was being considered for eligibility for special education, this is not documentation of a response to the specific intervention.

WHAT HAPPENS
IF YOU CAN'T DOCUMENT AN INTERVENTION EFFECT?

It is important to ask at this point what one is to do if experimental control is not established. In such a case, one can never say that a special intervention resulted in any observed change. The course of action at this point depends heavily on the stakes of the case. In low-stakes cases, there is little need for experimental control. It will be important to continue to track the child to see whether the desired behavior change continues, but the role of the intervention is not necessary to nail down. In a high-stakes case, there is a real issue when the child responded to something, but not necessarily the intervention. In such a case, it will be important to continue to use SCD to examine the role of the intervention in order to determine what is controlling the target behavior. Given that with high-stakes cases the child will likely continue to need intensive intervention, it is worth the time and effort to use SCD to deepen the understanding of the case. Such an understanding is critical to future intervention selection.

USING QUANTITATIVE METRICS

Over the last few decades the use of quantitative estimates of effect (often referred to as *effect sizes*) as an alternative to visual analysis for SCD has received increased interest (Parker & Hagan-Burke, 2007). To date, while some focus has been given to individual cases (Shadish, Rindskopf, & Hedges, 2008), the primary goal of the development of defensible quantitative metrics has been to facilitate the analysis of large numbers of SCD studies. This type of research, typically called meta-analysis, is critical to draw conclusions about the effectiveness of specific interventions. In school psychology and special education there have been a number of recent meta-analyses of SCD publications, some of which use quantitative metrics (Burns, Codding, et al., 2010; Burns & Wagner, 2008; Codding, Burns, & Lukito, 2011; Fabiano et al., 2009; Parker, Vannest, & Brown, 2009), some of which are based on visual analysis (Maggin, Chafouleas, Goddard, & Johnson, 2011; Maggin, Johnson, Chafouleas, Ruberto, & Berggren, in press). Although the development of quantitative metrics for of SCD analysis is an important topic for researchers, at the level of applied practice the utility and current availably of such a statistic should is more questionable.

At the most basic level, we should consider why quantitative metrics have become a popular method for discussing traditional research findings. In group comparison research, the historic use of "significance testing" has been criticized as an observed difference that can be statistically significant yet have little real-life importance. While this concern and subsequent development of estimates of effect is logical in the case of group research, it is not analogous with SCD. SCD has no history with significance testing; rather, all data are collected, graphed, and presented in raw form. The meaning of the data is defined as a change in the target behavior of some importance to the teacher, parent, or other relevant individual. If, for example, a child decreases calling-out behavior from 10 times an hour to 5 times an hour, the intervention team that can contextualize the results must judge the importance of that finding. In contrast, it has been historically argued that quantitative estimates do not fully express the formative path of outcome data and can result in inappropriate conclusions (Salzberg, Strain, & Baer, 1987; White, 1987). Perhaps more important, at this time there is no agreed-upon method for computing quantitative estimates for SCD. It is understood that Cohen's d (Cohen, 1988), no-assumptions effect size (Busk & Serlin, 1992), percentage of nonoverlapping data (Scruggs, Mastropieri, & Casto, 1987), R^2 (Pearson, 2010), percent of all nonoverlapping data (Parker, Hagan-Burke, & Vannest, 2007), and hierarchical linear modeling (Maggin, Swaminathan, et al., 2011; Shadish & Rindskopf, 2007) all have limitations when used with SCD. Suffice to say, although there is considerable interest and research in the quantitative analysis of SCD, at this time there are no safe strategies to guide practice. As such, practitioners are encouraged to rely on visual analysis when considering an intervention effect. This method has been vetted over more than 30 years of peer review and successful use in applied practice.

WRAPPING UP DESIGN AND ANALYSIS

The purpose of Chapters 4 and 5 was to provide a concise review of the role of SCD and related analysis in a comprehensive RTI model. At the most basic level, SCD and analysis provide the opportunity for schools to more systematically consider the effect of intervention and its role in observed outcomes. Considering the importance of a child's documented response in an RTI service delivery model, we believe that our field should embrace a truly scientific approach with students in the greatest need. For education as a discipline, it is critical that not only EBI and assessment are included, but that experimental design and analysis also be a core element. We hope these chapters will useful for readers who are committed to embracing a complete scientific approach to education. Readers interested in a more in-depth review of this topic should see *Evaluating Educational Interventions: Using Single-Case Design to Measure Response to Intervention* by Riley-Tillman and Burns (2009).

> Considering the importance of a child's documented response to an RTI service delivery model, we believe that our field should embrace a truly scientific approach with students in the greatest need.

Intervention Graph (Percent)

Student Name: _____   Interventionist: _____

Dates: _____   Setting: _____

Intervention: _____

_____

Outcome Data: _____

_____

Intervention Goal: _____

_____

Comments: _____

_____

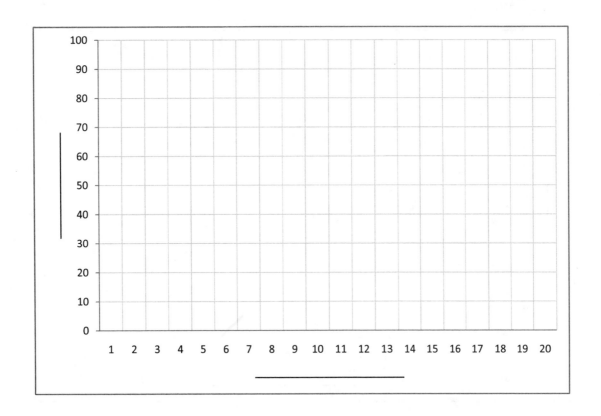

From T. Chris Riley-Tillman, Matthew K. Burns, and Kimberly Gibbons (2013). Copyright by The Guilford Press. Permission to photocopy this form is granted to purchasers of this book for personal use only (see copyright page for details). Purchasers can download additional copies of this form from *www.guilford.com/riley-forms*.

FORM 5.2

Intervention Graph (Frequency Count)

Student Name: _____   Interventionist: _____

Dates: _____   Setting: _____

Intervention: _____

_____

Outcome Data: _____

_____

Intervention Goal: _____

_____

Comments: _____

_____

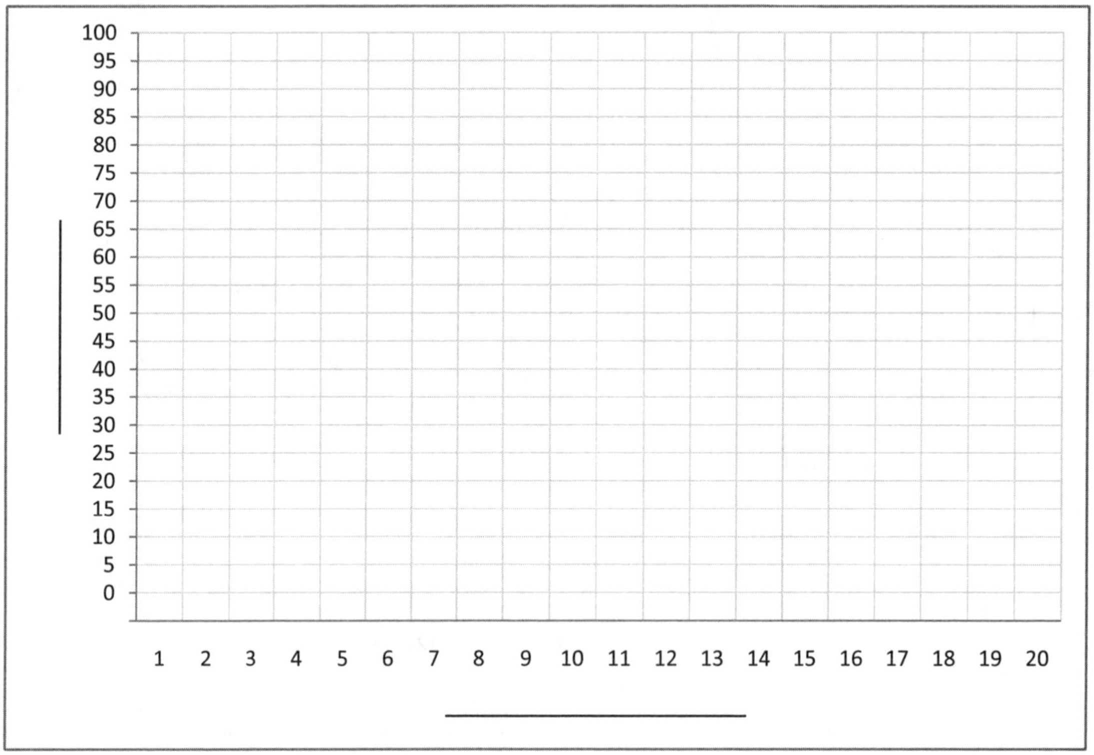

From T. Chris Riley-Tillman, Matthew K. Burns, and Kimberly Gibbons (2013). Copyright by The Guilford Press. Permission to photocopy this form is granted to purchasers of this book for personal use only (see copyright page for details). Purchasers can download additional copies of this form from *www.guilford.com/riley-forms*.

FORM 5.3

Multiple-Baseline Across-Targets Intervention Graphs

Student Name: _____   Interventionist: _____

Dates: _____   Setting: _____

Intervention: _____

_____

Outcome Data: _____

_____

Intervention Goal: _____

_____

Multiple-Baseline Targets: _____

_____

_____

(continued)

From T. Chris Riley-Tillman, Matthew K. Burns, and Kimberly Gibbons (2013). Copyright by The Guilford Press. Permission to photocopy this form is granted to purchasers of this book for personal use only (see copyright page for details). Purchasers can download additional copies of this form from *www.guilford.com/riley-forms*.

Multiple-Baseline Across-Targets Intervention Graph (Frequency Count)

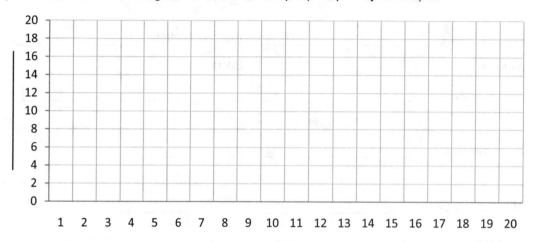

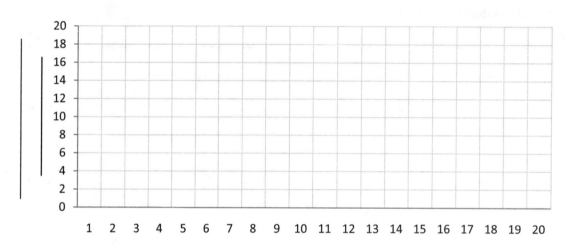

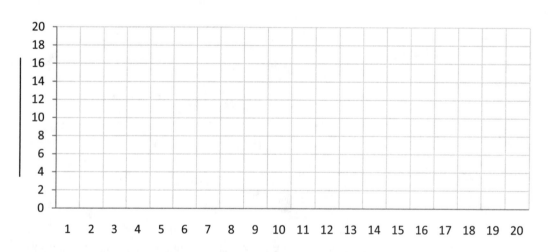

(continued)

Multiple-Baseline Across-Targets Intervention Graph (Percent)

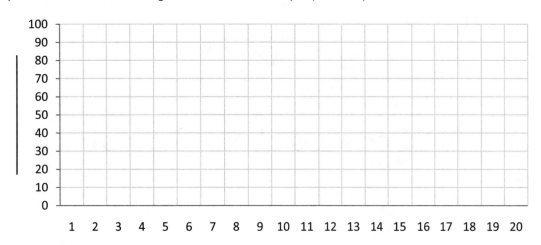

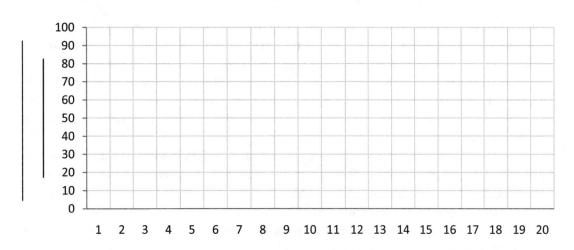

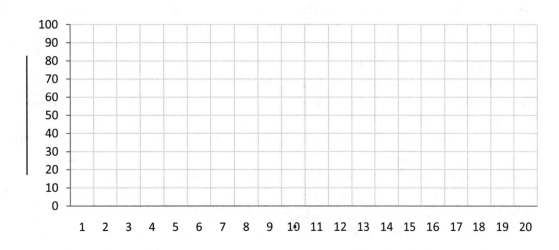

CHAPTER 6

Decisions about Groups

In an ideal world, each student would receive an individualized intervention delivered in a one-on-one setting with unlimited human resources of certified teachers and behavior specialists. Unfortunately, this utopian school does not exist, and in fact resources are becoming scarcer and scarcer, which suggests that efficiency is becoming increasingly important. The reason that we focus on RTI as a resource allocation model is because schools must put their dwindling resources where they will do the most good, and those decisions are best made with data.

Efficiency is an important consideration in designing RTI models, but it is more critical in Tier 2 than in Tier 3. In other words, we suggest that the primary focus of Tier 3 is effectiveness. In Tier 3, school personnel should dedicate considerable resources to assure student learning—"do whatever it takes." However, the primary focus in Tier 2 should be efficiency, in that we want to help as many students as we can. School personnel should recognize that there *will* inevitably be some students who do not perform well enough while receiving a Tier 2 intervention, and thus some students require a Tier 3 intervention. It is critical that schools reserve resources for supporting those intensive cases in Tier 3.

The second author recently consulted with a second-grade teacher who was engaged in in-depth analysis for all of her students and delivering individualized interventions for each. It was an impressive model, and the student outcome data were equally inspiring. We discussed several less intensive approaches to problem analysis in order to streamline her considerable efforts. The teacher became somewhat defensive and kept referring back to her strong student data. After several back-and-forth exchanges, she was asked about the potential for sustainability: "The data are great and your students are doing well, but can you keep this up for 5, 10, 20 years?" To which she replied, "Oh my gosh, no."

The example above is a common error in practice. Essentially, this well-meaning and highly skilled teacher was conducting Tier 3 analyses for Tier 1, which is only possible in the aforementioned utopian school. Thus school personnel should conduct lower-level analyses that were outlined in Chapter 2. The primary problem analysis question for Tier 1 is "Is there a classwide problem?" For Tier 2, the primary problem analysis question is "What is the category of the problem?" Schools that examine causal variables for more than 20% of their student population are engaging in Tier 3 analyses at Tier 1, which is not sustainable. In this chapter we talk about analyses conducted at Tiers 1 and 2 and focus on decision-making criteria.

We have continuously stated, and will do so again here, that the grade-level team (GLT) makes decisions in Tier 1 and 2 (and to some extent in Tier 3). Three times each year GLTs examine universal screening data and should use these questions to guide the conversation:

1. Is there a classwide problem?
   a. What is the median score for each classroom?
   b. Does the median score fall below the criterion?
2. Who needs a Tier 2 intervention (i.e., which students fall within the at-risk range)?
3. Are there any surprises or students whom we missed?
4. Among students identified as needing a Tier 2 intervention, what is the category of the problem?
5. Does anyone need Tier 3 right now?

Below we discuss questions within the context of group decisions made for Tier 1 and Tier 2, and how to use data to answer them.

TIER 1: IS THERE A CLASSWIDE PROBLEM?

Research has consistently demonstrated that the first step in identifying individual students with significant difficulties is to rule out the effect of a classwide problem (VanDerHeyden & Burns, 2005; VanDerHeyden, Witt, & Naquin, 2003). Consider the data presented in Table 6.1, which are based on data obtained from a group of third-grade students. Assume that any student whose oral reading fluency (ORF) score falls at or below 62 words correct per minute (WCPM) needs a Tier 2 intervention. All of the scores that repre-

> **Research has consistently demonstrated that the first step in identifying individual students with significant difficulties is to rule out the effect of a classwide problem.**

sented a student needing additional support are presented in bold text. Of the 23 students, 13 of them require a Tier 2 intervention. Is it possible to run a small-group (Tier 2) intervention for 13 of 23 students? Only in our utopian school could we implement a small-group intervention for that many students. More important, we likely have a situation where the students are not benefiting from core instruction.

Screening data are collected for each student three times per year. The data in Table 6.1 were from the January screening. After the data are collected, the data management team (see Chapter 2) makes sure that the data are arranged in a comprehensive manner. We suggest that every teacher receives a list like the one in Table 6.1 that includes the screening score for every student in her class. If more than one screener is used (e.g., ORF and measures of academic progress), then both scores would appear for each student. While

TABLE 6.1. Sample Classwide ORF Data

Student	ORF January 15	Percent correct January 15	ORF January 29	Percent correct January 29
Student 1	**37**	78%	**51**	88%
Student 2	129	95%	122	100%
Student 3	108	99%	126	98%
Student 4	**44**	93%	82	95%
Student 5	99	95%	102	99%
Student 6	**60**	94%	77	97%
Student 7	**25**	81%	**51**	85%
Student 8	**55**	93%	84	97%
Student 9	**49**	94%	80	94%
Student 10	76	98%	102	99%
Student 11	**60**	95%	83	98%
Student 12	**55**	93%	71	95%
Student 13	**56**	94%	90	98%
Student 14	135	100%	152	100%
Student 15	123	100%	143	100%
Student 16	83	98%	115	99%
Student 17	144	100%	150	99%
Student 18	101	100%	114	99%
Student 19	**40**	90%	**59**	94%
Student 20	**31**	75%	**51**	86%
Student 21	136	98%	141	100%
Student 22	**60**	93%	87	97%
Student 23	**30**	80%	**49**	89%
Median	**60**		87	

Note. Scores below the 62 WCPM criterion are in **bold**.

more recent, there is also increasing potential for behavior screening as discussed in depth in Volume 1.

The median screener score should also appear on the printout that each teacher receives. As stated earlier, the median is used or the class because a group of 30 or fewer scores is considered a small data set that is susceptible to outliers. However, it may also be appropriate to include a grade-level mean. If each classroom has approximately 25 students, then that is too small to report an average because one or two students reading 200 WCPM or 10 WCPM could really distort the average. However, if there are three classrooms per grade with 25 students in each, then GLTs can be much more confident in an average score with 75 students.

Criteria for Class Median

The class median in Table 6.1 is 60 WCPM. In our experience, it seems that very few GLTs adequately consider those data. The first step in implementing a tiered system of support is to examine the effects of quality core instruction, which can be grossly estimated by looking at the class median for the screening data. After finding the class median, the score can then be compared to some national or meaningful criterion, or school personnel can compute criteria themselves.

Normative Criteria

Schools using the Aimsweb (Pearson, 2010) or Dynamic Indicators of Basic Early Literacy Skills (DIBELS) systems can simply compare the class median to the criterion suggested by that particular system. However, national norms are available for ORF for those without either system at *www.readnaturally.com/howto/orftable.htm*. We suggest using the 25th percentile as the criterion because it represents the lowest end of the average range, but many schools could use the 50th percentile if that is more appropriate. Schools using other norm-referenced group measures of math and reading (e.g., Measures of Academic Progress for Math, Measures of Academic Progress for Reading, STAR Math, STAR Reading) could also compare the class median to the 25th percentile on a national norm.

Instructional-Level Criteria

We discussed the concept of instructional level in Chapter 3, and so will only provide a brief review here. There is some debate about how best to determine an instructional level, but recent research found that Gickling and Thompson (1985) criteria of 93–97% known results is better for decisions than other approaches for reading (Parker, Burns, & McComas, 2012). For example, Deno and Mirkin (1977) suggested criteria of 40–60 WCPM (first and second grade) and 70–100 WCPM (third to sixth grade), but those criteria were derived from experience in one school in Minnesota (S. L. Deno, personal communication, April 15, 2005), which suggests limited utility in other districts across the country. The Gickling and Thompson (1985) criteria are well researched, but have not been validated for the purpose of identifying classwide problems. Thus using the instructional level as a criterion to identify classwide problems in reading makes some intuitive sense given that it is a potentially meaningful criterion, but more research is needed before that can happen with confidence.

There is research to support the use of instructional-level criteria to identify classwide problems for math. Deno and Mirkin (1977) presented fluency criteria to determine an instructional level for math of 21–40 digits correct per minute (DCPM) for students in first through third grade and 41–80 DCPM for fourth through 12th grade, but just like the criteria for reading, those estimates were not derived from empirical research. A study conducted by Burns and colleagues (2006) found instructional-level criteria for math of 14–31 DCPM for second and third graders, and 24–49 DCPM for fourth- and fifth-grade students.

Therefore a class median less than 14 DCPM for students in second and third grade, and less than 24 DCPM for fourth and fifth graders would suggest a classwide problem.

Computing the Criterion

The easiest option for classwide problem identification is probably using a national norm, but there are better and more complex options. For example, a district could use its own data and correlate those scores with state accountability test scores and build a regression formula from the results to find the benchmark score that best predicts a passing score on the state test. Alternatively, a district could conduct a receiver operating characteristics (ROC) curve analysis to determine which score predicts a passing score on the state test.

To conduct an ROC analysis, school personnel need only record the screening score for each student and a dichotomous state variable for the state test (i.e., pass or fail). An ROC analysis can then be computed by someone with moderate proficiency in statistical analyses. The following steps allow for an ROC analysis within SPSS statistical software package:

1. Arrange the data in a row with one column (variable) being the screening score for each student and one being the state of the criterion (e.g., 1 = passed the state test, and 0 = failed the state test).
2. Select Analyze from the top menu.
3. Select ROC Analysis.
4. At the ROC Curve Window that pops up, select the screening measure as the Test Variable and the criterion variable state as the State Variable.
5. When you enter a State Variable, you will be prompted to add the Value of the State Variable, which asks what value would be the desired outcome. In this case, enter the value that you assigned to passing the state test (e.g., 1).
6. In the Display section of the pop-up window, select Coordinate Points of the ROC Curve.
7. Click OK, and an output file will appear.
8. Examine the Coordinates of the Curve table, which has three headings: Positive if Greater than or Equal to, Sensitivity, and 1-Specificity. Find the Sensitivity value of .70 in the middle column and find the score in the left column that represents a sensitivity of .70.
9. If the 1-Specificity value is approximately .3 for the value that you have identified, then that score would likely be an acceptable criterion to which screening data can be compared. If not, then adjust the score up or down until 1-Specificity equals roughly .70, but remember to keep the emphasis on Sensitivity because that is the value that prevents false negatives (suggested that no additional support was needed when it actually was).

Although an ROC analysis is not complicated, it may exceed the skills of some practitioners, and some may not have access to SPSS. An easier alternative is to include screening and state test scores in a Microsoft Excel file and compute a simple regression. We start with the following basic regression equation:

$$Y = a + bX$$

where Y is the criterion being predicted (passing the state test score), a is the intercept of the two sets of data (the score on Y when X is 0), b is the slope of the line that intersects the two sets of data, and X is the independent variable (e.g., screening score). Unlike an ROC analysis, the actual state test score is used rather than a dichotomous score (e.g., 1 and 0), but the test score would be the lowest score that represents a passing score. The data for each student would be entered into an Excel file, with one column being the score on the screener and a second column being the state test score. Next, we use simple algebraic procedures to convert the equation above, which is configured to determine X when Y is a proficient test score, resulting in the following equation:

$$X = (Y - a)/b$$

If we assume that a passing score is 200, then Y would equal 200, but we still need a (intercept) and b (slope). Both of these values can be easily determined in Excel with the SLOPE and INTERCEPT functions, in which the state test score is the dependent variable and the screening score is the independent variable. To find the slope (b) and intercept (a), simply use the function wizard (SLOPE and INTERCEPT) and enter in the array with the state test scores as the "dependent numerical data" and the screening scores as the "independent numerical data." Slope represents the relationship between the two sets of data and intercept is the value of the dependent score if the independent score was 0. If we assume that the slope value from our data = .20 and the intercept = 180.50, then the values for the equation above are $X = (200[Y] - 180.50[a])/.20[b])$, which yields a score of 97.5 and suggests that a score of 97.5 would predict that the student would pass the state test and those who score less than that would require remediation.

The resulting criteria from either approach described above would have the advantage of being local and directly linked to accountability tests, but should be validated through estimates of sensitivity and specificity. Both of these options are relatively simple and easily implemented if the district has personnel trained in statistical methodologies (e.g., a research and evaluation department or director); if not, then districts may wish to use the national norm option.

Summary

We suggested that any student in Table 6.1 scoring at or below 62 WCPM would require a Tier 2 intervention. We selected that number because the national norms referenced above indicated that 62 WCPM represented the 25th percentile for the third-grade winter benchmark using ORF. The class median fell below our criterion and suggested a classwide problem.

The GLT examined the data in Table 6.1 and concluded that they needed to (1) examine their core instructional practices, (2) implement a classwide intervention, and (3) monitor progress every other week. We discussed the classwide intervention in detail in Volume 1 and will not do so here, but the protocol uses partner reading and paragraph shrinking as outlined by the Peer Assisted Learning Strategies (Fuchs & Fuchs, 1998). Each student was then assessed with a different grade-level ORF 2 weeks later, the results of which are also in Table 6.1. The intervention and data collection continued until the class median exceeded the criterion (62 WCPM, 79 WCPM for AIMSweb, 67 WCPM for DIBELS), which happened after only 2 weeks.

VanDerHeyden and colleagues (VanDerHeyden & Burns, 2005; VanDerHeyden et al., 2003) have consistently demonstrated the importance of identifying and remediating a classwide problem, and the example in Table 6.1 demonstrates it as well. Recall that 13 of the 23 students required a Tier 2 intervention before the classwide intervention occurred. However, after only 2 weeks of partner reading and paragraph shrinking for 20 minutes each day, only five of the students fell below our criterion and required intervention. The five students represent 22% of the classroom, which is consistent with recommendations of 80% Tier 1 and 20% Tier 2 (Batche, Elliott, et al., 2006). Moreover, now the number of students needing intervention is far more manageable for GLTs to implement a multi-tiered system of support, starting with Tier 2.

TIER 2

If no classwide problems exist, or if they have been successfully remediated, then the GLTs can move on to answer additional questions regarding Tier 2. Below we discuss the remaining four questions outlined above and how to answer each.

Who Needs a Tier 2 Intervention?

After ruling or factoring out a classwide problem, individual students can then be identified for additional intervention in Tier 2. There are two options to do so. First, if there are no classwide problems, then school personnel can simply identify the lowest 25% of each grade level. For example, 25% of the students in Table 6.1 would be six students, which would be Students 1, 7, 12, 19, 20, and 23. All but Student 12 would be identified as needing an intervention simply by selecting students who fell below our criterion. We have found that after eliminating all classwide problems, then the number of students identified as needing support is roughly the same for either approach. However, it is important to note that this should be a grade-level decision rather than a classroom one. Our example in Table 6.1 is from one classroom, but once classwide problems are eliminated, then the decision about who receives a Tier 2 intervention should be made with grade data (i.e., lowest 25% of the grade rather than a classroom).

> **If there are no classwide problems, then school personnel can simply identify the lowest 25% of each grade level.**

If more than one source of data is collected at benchmark (e.g., letter-sound fluency and letter-naming fluency in kindergarten), then students at or below the 25th percentile for each score would be identified, and those who fall into that category on both scores would be targeted first. If there were three scores, than those that fell below the 25th percentile on all three would be targeted first, and those within that lowest quartile on two scores would be added until 25% of the student population was reached (e.g., two classrooms of second graders with 25 in each one would result in 10 students being identified for Tier 2).

Any Surprises or Missed Students?

After identifying who needs a Tier 2 intervention, students "at the margins" should be examined next. The data in Table 6.1 suggest that five students need a Tier 2 intervention. However, GLTs would be wise to examine the data for Student 6 (77 WCPM) and Student 12 (71 WCPM). They are both above our criterion of 62 WCPM, but the team should make sure that these are not false negatives, or are students who need intervention but who do not score as such. Classroom data should be examined, but the GLT could also dive somewhat deeper into screening data.

As mentioned above, 93–97% words read correctly is well-researched criterion for the instructional level. GLTs could examine the percentage of items correctly completed to help interpret the data. For example, Students 6 and 12 both read at least 93% of the words correctly, which could confirm that they have demonstrated reading skills sufficient not to warrant a Tier 2 intervention. Of course, if multiple pieces of data are used within the screening process, then all data should be considered. Finally, classroom data can be very helpful to determine whether a student who scores above the cutoff actually does require intervention. Classroom teachers should bring their running records, word list assessments, math-fact assessments, and so on, to help inform the conversation.

In addition to discussing students who may have been falsely identified as not needing an intervention, GLTs should discuss students who may have been misidentified as needing an intervention. In our experience, the correspondence between screening data and teacher observations is quite high, but we often hear teachers say something like "He scored that low? Oh, I remember *that* day." GLTs can question the validity of the screening data if there is a legitimate reason to do so and can simply conduct a second screening now if needed.

What Intervention Is Appropriate?: Category of Deficit

Thus far we have talked about examining individual student data to make decisions about individual students. However, the next step (and question) is for the GLT to use data to group the students to receive interventions. Interventions are more effective if they correctly target the skill deficit (Burns, VanDerHeyden, & Boice, 2008). The National Reading Panel (2000) reported four areas necessary for reading instruction—phonemic awareness, phonics, reading fluency, and vocabulary/comprehension—that could serve as the basis for a low-level analysis for reading intervention. As discussed in Chapter 3, once screening data suggest a difficulty, more specific subskill mastery measures would be used to identify the specific skill deficit and resulting intervention.

Phonemic awareness can be assessed with phoneme segmentation fluency and initial sound fluency, or standardized measures such as the Comprehensive Test of Phonological Processing (CTOPP; Wagner, Torgesen, & Rashotte, 1999). Reading fluency is pretty straightforward because most school districts use ORF as the benchmark score in grades 2 through 6. However, the Test of Silent Contextual Reading Fluency (TSCRF; Hammill, Wiederhold, & Allen, 2006) is a group-administered assessment that purportedly measures reading fluency, and previous research found that it effectively identified reading fluency deficits for individual students (Burns et al., 2012). There are several options for assessing phonics (also called decoding or alphabetic principle) including letter-sound or letter-word name fluency, and nonsense word fluency, the scores for which could be compared to standards associated with DIBELS (see *dibels.uoregon.edu/benchmarkgoals.pdf*). Moreover, there are several standardized norm-referenced measures such as the Word Attack (WA) subtest of the Woodcock–Johnson Tests of Achievement or any standardized word attack subtest. Norm-referenced data obtained from standardized measures like the CTOPP, TSCRF, or WA subtests could be compared to the 25th percentile to determine a deficit. Scores that fall below the 25th percentile suggest a deficit in that particular skill.

> **Interventions are more effective if they correctly target the skill deficit.**

The data presented could also provide some indication about potential interventions. There were five students who scored below our criterion of 62 WCPM on the January 29 assessment. The accuracy data are presented in the next column and can be compared to the instructional level criterion of 93–97%. All but one student (Student 19) who scored below 62 WCPM read fewer than 93% of the words correctly, which could suggest that these students are struggling to break the code. Thus Student 19 would likely benefit from a fluency-oriented intervention (e.g., repeated reading), but the other four students would likely benefit from a decoding intervention. Certainly GLTs can conduct one of the decoding interventions mentioned above to confirm the need for a decoding intervention, but quickly examining the accuracy data could suggest a potential starting point.

The code-based aspects of reading (phonemic awareness, phonics, and reading fluency) are easily measured, but reading comprehension is more complex. Perhaps the most straightforward way to include comprehension data within the problem-analysis framework is to utilize a group-administered measure of reading comprehension such as the Measures of Academic Progress for Reading (MAP-R; Northwest Evaluation Association, 2003) or STAR-Reading (Renaissance Learning, 2011). Again, students who score below the 25th percentile on a group-administered measure would likely struggle with comprehension.

Putting the data from the National Reading Panel (2000) instructional areas can suggest a target for the intervention by working backward through the process to find the root of the problem. Children who are struggling readers tend to follow a somewhat sequential approach in that phonemic awareness is needed before they can decode, decoding is needed before they can read fluently, and fluent reading is needed before they can comprehend what they read (Berninger, Abbott, Vermeulen, & Fulton, 2006). Thus practitioners can work backward in the sequence in the following manner:

1. A student who has low comprehension but sufficient fluency would likely benefit from a comprehension intervention.
2. A student with low comprehension and low fluency, but acceptable decoding, would likely require a fluency intervention.
3. A student who struggles with comprehension, fluency, and decoding, but who demonstrates sufficient phonemic awareness, would likely require a decoding intervention.
4. Finally, a student who is low in all areas would require a phonemic awareness intervention.

Identifying the category of the problem for math is somewhat more straightforward, but is much more specific. The categories for math instruction are not as well established as they are for reading. According to the National Research Council, math proficiency is composed of (1) conceptual understanding, (2) procedural fluency, (3) ability to formulate and mentally represent problems, (4) reasoning, and (5) and successful application of math to daily activities (Kilpatrick, Swafford, & Finell, 2001). The National Mathematics Advisory Panel (2008) recommended that math instruction simultaneously develop conceptual understanding, computational fluency, and problem-solving skills. Thus there are categories, but their link to intervention is less clear.

Alternatively, GLTs could use the scope and sequence of their local curriculum to find the category of the problem for math. For example, the sample of skills listed in Table 6.2 is taken from VanDerHeyden and Burns (2009), who found an instructional sequence for math objectives that accurately predicted success in math. The sequence in the table will be used as a sample sequence for this example, but GLTs could apply this process to the objectives for their grade-appropriate curriculum. After being identified as needing additional support on a group-administered math test (e.g., STAR-Math), each student completes a series of single-skill assessments. Fortunately, these diagnostic assessments can be developed ahead of time, and only a few different forms are needed for each one.

Single-skill assessments in math are referred to as subskill mastery measures (SSMs) and can be constructed, administered, and scored as a curriculum-based measurement (CBM; see Chapter 3). Teachers can select published math CBM probes (e.g. AIMSweb), use a Web-based system to create one (e.g., *www.mathfactscafe.com*), or create their own. Math CBM probes usually contain at least 25 problems depending on the curriculum difficulty (Fuchs & Fuchs, 1991; Hosp, Hosp, & Howell, 2007). After constructing the probes, students are given 2 or 4 minutes to complete as many items as they can (Christ, Johnson-Gros, & Hintze, 2005). Administration consists of providing the student the sheet to be completed and asking them to (1) begin with the first problem and work across the page, (2) place an *X* over problems that they cannot complete, and (3) to keep working until they complete the page or are told to stop (Shinn, 1989). After 4 minutes the administration stops and the probe is collected for scoring.

TABLE 6.2. Sample of Math Objectives Based on VanDerHeyden and Burns (2009).

Third grade	Fourth grade
1. Addition and subtraction 0–20	1. Multiplication facts 0–12
2. Fact families addition and subtraction 0–20	2. Division facts 0–12
3. Three-digit addition with and without regrouping	3. Double/triple digit multiplied by single digit
4. Three-digit subtraction with and without regrouping	4. Double digit multiplied by double digit without regrouping
5. Multiplication facts 0–9	5. Double digit multiplied by double digit with regrouping
6. Division facts 0–9	6. Single-digit divisor into double-digit dividend without remainder
7. Addition and subtraction of fractions with like denominators	7. Single-digit divisor into double-digit dividend with remainder
8. Double/triple digit multiplied by single digit	8. Single-/double-digit divisor into single-/double-digit dividend without remainders
9. Single digit divided into double/triple digit without remainders	9. Addition and subtraction of fractions with like denominators
10. Addition and subtraction of decimals to the hundredths place	10. Multiplication of multidigit numbers by multidigit numbers
	11. Addition and subtraction of decimals to the hundredths place

As discussed in Chapter 3, CBM math probes provide fluency scores measured in DCPM, which makes the data more sensitive to change than measuring the number of correct answers (Hosp et al., 2007). In order to determine DCPM, the total number of digits correct in the probe is divided by the length of the administration (e.g., 60 digits correct in a 4-minute administration would result in 15 DCPM). The number of DCPM can be interpreted by comparing them to standards derived by Burns and colleagues (2006) of 14–31 DCPM for second and third grade, and 24–49 DCPM for fourth and fifth grade. It is unclear what standards to use for older students, but the 24–49 DCPM may be effective for somewhat older grades, and a criterion of 90% correct may be useful for students in middle and high school.

In our example, we would start with skill number 10 for third graders (add and subtract decimals to the hundredths place) and would administer a single-skill probe. We would then continue to administer single-skill probes in a backward sequence (e.g., skill 9—double/triple digit multiplied by single digit; skill 8—single digit divided into double/triple digit without remainder) until the student's score fell within the instructional-level range of 14–31 DCPM, and that would be our starting point for the category of the problem. Students could then receive a fluency-based intervention as a Tier 2 intervention. We discussed the actual interventions in Volume 1, but research has supported this process of finding the skill and implementing a fluency-based remediation (Burns et al., 2012; VanDerHeyden & Burns, 2005).

As discussed extensively in Volume 1, there is a consistent group of functions (e.g., skill deficit, attention seeking, escape) that are the base of behavior problems. While considering behavioral function is typically thought to be useful at the level of the individual child, it can apply to groups as well. For example, if a cluster of children exhibits a consistent attention-seeking behavior with the teacher, a group intervention is more likely to be effective than trying to develop multiple individual plans. In addition, group interventions like the Good Behavior Game (Barrish, Saunders, & Wolf, 1969) can capitalize on the group format to assess both peer and teacher attention. This topic was addressed in depth throughout Volume 1, and that book should be consulted for more discussion and intervention suggestions.

Once the target skill is identified, then the students can be grouped according to the data. In reading, the students for whom comprehension was the root of the problem (i.e., the category of the problem) would be grouped together, as would students for whom fluency, decoding, and phonemic awareness was the primary issue. In math, the students who demonstrated an instructional-level skill level in common objectives (e.g., double/triple digit multiplied by single-digit) would be grouped together for intervention purposes. This same construct can be applied to behavior intervention as described above.

Is There Anyone for Whom We Should Go Right to Tier 3?

The focus of this chapter is on groups of students, but part of the process of answering questions within Tier 2 is to determine whether any students have such severe deficits that a Tier 3 intervention is immediately warranted. We again caution against triaging students into tiers of intervention (e.g., students scoring between the 10th and 25th percentile receive a Tier 2 intervention and those at or below the 9th percentile receive a Tier 3 intervention) based on recent meta-analytic research that questioned the practice (Burns & Scholin, in press). Instead of triaging students based on the level of preintervention scores, GLTs could consider other classroom data to decide whether students require a Tier 3 intervention, which we discuss more thoroughly in Chapter 7.

CHAPTER 7

Decisions about Individual Students

Well-meaning practitioners often select interventions without really thinking about why. Maybe the intervention is selected because it is one that the teacher is quite familiar with, has used before, makes intuitive sense, or is easy to use. All of these are acceptable factors to consider, but none of them assure that the intervention will actually work. Thus far in this book we have talked about identifying interventions for groups of students, but in this chapter we talk about making decisions for individual students within Tier 3. (Volume 1 and Chapters 2–5 in this volume provide a good deal of the theory and techniques for this stage of decision making.)

Recall from previous chapters that even with strong instruction, solid classroom management, a research-based curriculum, and effective Tier 2 practices, 5% of the students may require individualized interventions (Burns et al., 2005). At this stage of an RTI model, the problem-solving team (PST) comes into play. Grade-level teams (GLTs) examine data to evaluate the progress of students receiving Tier 2 intervention, and students for whom progress is not deemed adequate are referred to the PST. We suggest that *all* referrals to a PST go through a GLT, including behavioral difficulties, and that these decisions be made with

> **We suggest that *all* referrals to a PST go through a GLT, including behavioral difficulties, and that these decisions be made with data.**

data. Doing so will require the GLT to become more self-sufficient in examining data and designing interventions. For example, if multiple students exhibit the same difficulty and the PST selects the same intervention for each, then subsequent instances of the same or similar difficulties may be addressed by the GLT. This process reflects one of the core goals of an RTI model, which is to increase teacher and team skill though the problem-solving process. In other words, an effective PST process can actually reduce the number of students referred to the PST.

Once the GLT examines the monitoring data and decides that a referral is warranted, they then complete the referral form and send it to the PST. The PST should then implement the adopted problem-analysis framework (see Chapter 3) and immediately start compiling data. The process of compiling data often involves having a consultant from the team meet with the referring teacher to determine whether additional data are needed (see Burns, Wiley, & Viglietta, 2008, for a detailed description of this process). PSTs should almost never meet and then decide to stop the process in order to collect additional data to analyze the problem, and then reconvene 1 or 2 weeks later. Even 1 to 2 weeks can be a tremendous amount of wasted time when starting an intervention. At the end of the PST meeting, the team should decide what to target, what intervention to use, and how to monitor progress. Each of these is discussed below.

SELECTING AN INTERVENTION TARGET

As discussed in Chapter 3 and throughout Volume 1 we advocate for a skill-by-treatment approach that directly measures skills and requires very low-level inferences (Christ, 2008). Some PSTs rely on indirect and high-inference hypotheses associated with ambiguous and difficult-to-measure constructs (e.g., executive functioning), but a skills-by-treatment approach identifies the most relevant skill deficits to target for intervention.

The process described in Chapter 6 can be applied to individual students to determine the area in which the intervention should be targeted. First, PSTs have to select the broad category of math, reading, writing, or behavior. There are a few factors to consider, such as the urgency of the behavior or the potential for interfering with other student learning. Moreover, PSTs should consider keystone skills, or skills that would have the broadest implications. Reading often serves as a keystone skill because it can be linked to difficulties in math, writing, and behavior.

Within reading, the areas examined by the National Reading Panel (2000), and discussed in Chapter 3, could be conceived as a developmental framework for a reading intervention selection model. One of the first acts of the National Reading Panel was to divide reading into major topic areas, including alphabetics (phonemic awareness and phonics instruction), reading fluency, and comprehension (including vocabulary instruction and text comprehension instruction). Reading interventions can be targeted to students' needs within such a framework because each skill relies on at least basic proficiency of preceding skills before the next one can develop.

Math interventions rely more on specific objectives within a curriculum framework. GLTs could conduct single-skill assessments to determine student functioning in each objective. In relation to behavior, it will be important to obtain a full understanding of the topography of the behavior as well as the antecedents and consequence that support it. Fortunately, within a well-established RTI model, the first step of identifying the intervention target should already be accomplished because the category of the problem was identified in Tier 2 (see Chapter 6). However, PSTs must then go deeper to actually select the intervention.

SELECTING THE INTERVENTION

Once the appropriate target area is developed, learning theory can be used to focus intervention efforts more clearly using the learning hierarchy discussed in Chapter 3 and in Volume 1. Recall that the learning hierarchy (Haring & Eaton, 1978) suggests that students progress through four phases when learning a new skill: acquisition, proficiency, generalization, and adaptation. During the acquisition phase, when a student is first learning a skill, she is slow and makes a lot of errors. For example, in the development of reading fluency, a student in this stage reads very slowly and makes several errors in decoding individual words. With social behavior, a child first must first be taught the basic skills necessary for schooling, such as raising a hand to be called on rather than calling out. As with reading, there is an expectation that students will exhibit errors initially as prior methods of getting attention are attempted. Entering the proficiency phase, the student can perform the skill accurately but remains slow in execution; thus the aim of this phase is to increase the rate of accuracy. In the case of reading fluency, the student may be able to accurately decode words, but she still reads at a very slow word-by-word rate. With behavior, the student in this phase has the basic skill, but needs to increase consistency until the appropriate behavior becomes somewhat automatic. During the generalization phase, the student can quickly and accurately apply the skill within the context that it was learned, and she begins to apply the skill to a variety of materials and contexts. A student in the generalization phase of reading fluency may apply the skill to reading a variety of different types of text such as letters, poems, and even science texts. With behavior, the child will try out a skill learned in one setting in another. Finally, in the adaptation phase the student learns to extract and apply the abstract meaning or goal of the skill to new situations without direction; the learned skill may also be used for future development of new skills. In the case of reading fluency, the abstract goal of fluent reading is to decode the text in a reasonable amount of time so that the student can efficiently extract meaning from it. With behavior, adaptation is demonstrated when the child uses generalized skill to appropriately get attention in a fully different setting such as politely engaging in a dinner discussion rather than blurting out a question.

The learning hierarchy provides guidance on the types of instructional strategies that match students' learning needs at each stage. Interventions for students in the acquisition phase focus on building response accuracy and could include demonstration, modeling, guided practice, frequent feedback, and routine drill. Once children reach proficiency they benefit most from instruction designed to increase the rate of skill performance such as novel practice opportunities, which includes frequent opportunities to respond and reinforcement for fluent performance. It is important to note that this stage can take a long time and require intervention alteration based on the child. The goal of the later stages of learning (i.e., generalization and adaptation) is to use the mastered skill effectively across a variety of materials and contexts. Students at these stages may require different instructional strategies such as problem solving, discrimination/differentiation training, and practice to apply mastered skills under novel conditions and more complex tasks (Haring & Eaton,

1978). See Appendix 7.1 for brief team meeting forms designed to be utilized with this approach to intervention selection.

The appropriate phase of the learning hierarchy is identified by collecting data regarding the accuracy and fluency with which the skill is completed. How fluently a skill is completed is commonly accepted as an indicator of proficiency and frequently assessed with CBMs such as WCPM, DCPM, and correct letter sequences per minute. However, accuracy is less commonly examined despite the importance of those data. Betts (1946) first noted the importance of assessing how accurately a skill is performed by reporting that a student must be able to automatically recognize about 95% of the words while reading in order for comprehension to occur. Subsequent research found that when students can effortlessly read between 93 and 97% of the words, they not only comprehend well, but also spend more time on task and complete a greater percentage of the activity than when they work with material that is too difficult (less than 93% known) or too easy (more than 97% known) (Gickling & Armstrong, 1978; Treptow et al., 2007). For other nonreading tasks, sometimes called drill tasks (e.g., spelling, phonics, sight-word recognition; Gickling & Thompson, 1985), a different set of instructional-level criteria have been indicated, suggesting that 90% known items be included in the learning stimulus set (Burns, 2004). Thus students who complete a reading task with less than 90–93% accuracy require explicit instruction in the task, modeling, and immediate error correction. Those who still work slowly but complete more than 90% of the items (e.g., 93% of the words read correctly or 90% of the correct letter sounds given) require additional practice with the items followed by immediate feedback.

MONITORING PROGRESS

Recent advances in learning theory discussed throughout this book and Volume 1 allow us to hypothesize which intervention will be successful with more accuracy than in the past. However, we never know in advance whether an intervention that has been effective with groups of students will be effective with an *individual* student. Likewise, functional assessment/analysis theory has provided an understanding that intervention analysis cannot end after functional assessment. Rather, it is essential to go through the analysis process to examine whether the intervention selected is effective. While using EBIs certainly increases the likelihood of positive student outcomes, providing feedback to teachers on student responsiveness to intervention also has a powerful impact on student outcomes. Below we discuss the logistics of monitoring progress and how to collect and use the data.

Logistics of Strategic and Intensive Measurement

All students who receive Tier 2 or Tier 3 interventions will need to have their progress monitored more frequently than three times per year. We also suggest that students who stopped receiving intervention because of success (i.e., scored above benchmark standards) still be assessed on a less frequent basis than those currently receiving intervention but more frequently than triannually.

Identify Who Will Collect Data

A variety of school staff may collect progress-monitoring data. Some buildings use reading teachers, regular education teachers, special education teachers, paraprofessionals, and/or volunteers to assist in data collection. When paraprofessionals and volunteers are used, it is important that their role be restricted to data collection versus data interpretation. Teachers should always be responsible for examining the data often and applying rules to make instructional decisions. While there is not a standard rule, we have found that the most efficient way to collect data is to develop a schedule with the names of all students in a grade level to be monitored, dates (or days of the week) of monitoring, and who is responsible for conducting the monitoring. Developing a formal progress-monitoring schedule helps ensure that data are collected with the intended frequency.

Identify Measurement Material

Many schools select the material with which to monitor progress by just using whatever is available within the monitoring system without giving much thought to the process. The result of a formulaic monitoring system is often a mismatch between assessment and intervention. Moreover, it may not be possible to make all necessary decisions with just one source of data.

As discussed in Chapter 2, progress should be monitored with a general outcome measure (GOM) and an indicator of the specific skill for the intervention target (subskill mastery measure). Table 2.1 provides examples of psychometrically sound GOM and subskill measures. Curriculum-based measures of oral reading fluency (CBM-R) can be an effective GOM for reading for most grades, but only if written at the student's grade level. If entitlement decisions are being made, it is imperative to use grade-level passages to determine the degree of discrepancy in both level and rate of growth compared to same-age peers. However, instructional-level passages can also provide useful data, and Gibbons and Howe (2000) found a lower standard error of measurement and greater sensitivity using progress monitoring materials one grade above the student's instructional level. Instructional level can be determined by sampling reading passages for 1 minute and computing the percentage of words read correctly per minute: (number of words read correctly/total number of words) × 100. The percentage can then be compared to the instructional level criteria of 93–99% correct (Gickling & Thompson, 1985). Please see Chapter 3 for more information about assessing a child's current instructional level.

It may not be appropriate to use instructional level CBM-R to monitor progress for students in kindergarten and first grade, or even with older students receiving decoding interventions. It may be beneficial to monitor progress with a grade-level CBM-R as the GOM, but to use decoding measures such as nonsense-word fluency, letter-sound fluency, or word lists that focus on specific decoding skills. The Minnesota Center for Reading Research developed several specific skill measures for reading that can be downloaded and used for free at *www.cehd.umn.edu/reading/PRESS/resources/assessment.html*.

Monitoring progress is somewhat more straightforward for math because skill measures are more easily developed, which is described in Chapter 3. GOM measures for math should include multiskill assessments that address the objectives within a grade-level curriculum. Skill measures within math assess single skills from the curriculum objectives. However, math application measures tend to have lower reliability than computation probes and are less sensitive to growth.

For behavior, there are a number of developing options. Direct behavior rating (DBR) was developed to provide progress monitoring data for behavior intervention (Chafouleas et al., 2009). The most researched version of DBR, the Direct Behavior Rating—Single Item Scale (DBR-SIS), provides data on academic engagement, disruptive behavior, and respectful behavior as well as some options for specific targets. For more information on DBR see *www.directbeahviorratings.org*. Systematic direct observation (SDO) also provides a highly reliable method to monitor progress (Chafouleas, Riley-Tillman, & Sugai, 2007). With a long history of use in the field, SDO is considered defensible and has flexible options for selecting target behaviors.

Identify How Often Data Will Be Collected

> **As student needs dictate progressively more intensive services, measurement becomes more frequent.**

When determining the frequency of data collection, it is helpful to consider severity of student need. Progress is usually monitored either monthly or biweekly for students at Tier 2, and either weekly or twice weekly for students at Tier 3. As student needs dictate progressively more intensive services, measurement becomes more frequent. For example, with intensive behavior problems it is not uncommon to need daily progress monitoring.

Set Ambitious Goals

Once the appropriate measurement material is identified, the last logistical decision is to set a goal for each student. All goals should have the following four components specified: (1) a time frame, (2) the measurement conditions, (3) the desired behavior, and (4) a criterion for success. Using these components, a template for wording of the goal statement is as follows: "In [time frame] weeks, when [conditions] occur, [learner] will [behavior] to [criterion]."

TIME FRAME

When setting a time frame for the goal, teams can select options such as the end of the year, end of semester, certain number of weeks, or the next benchmark data collection window. We recommend a long-term goal (e.g, the end of the school year) so that teams do not have to meet and reset goals with each new intervention. When selecting short-term goals, it is important to give the intervention long enough to work and allow for the team to gather enough data to make valid decisions.

MEASUREMENT CONDITIONS

The measurement conditions for academic skills typically are the grade level of the materials (e.g., third-grade reading passages) and the type of materials used (e.g., AIMSweb, DIBELS, Read Naturally, Houghton-Mifflin). The measurement conditions for behavioral goals typically are based on direct observation in a particular setting (reading class, playground, school bus, all school settings, etc.). The behavior for academic goals typically are that students will read, solve math problems, write, or spell. In the area of behavior, it is recommended that teams focus on increasing positive replacement behaviors rather than decreasing negative behavior. Examples of target behaviors may be following instructions, accepting no for an answer, asking for help, or active engagement during instruction.

CRITERION FOR SUCCESS

The criterion for success is a statement of the final level of expected performance (e.g., 49 WCPM by the spring of first grade). In academic areas, the criterion for success is typically the year-end target score for that grade level in the specific skill area. In the area of behavior, teams may consider a 10% improvement of the behavioral skill per week. Research clearly indicates that student performance is maximized when teachers set ambitious goals. Table 7.1 provides some growth estimates in basic skill areas for various grade levels based on research. Table 7.2 displays how much growth typical students need to make at the St. Croix River Education District in order to have an 80% chance of performing proficiently on statewide assessments. These data provide educators with a starting point for goal setting; however, it is important to remember that students who are at risk need to make more progress than typical peers to close the achievement gap.

In summary, to check that all the logistical factors in progress monitoring have been addressed, teams should discuss whether they have determined how data will be collected, what materials will be used, who will collect data, when data will be collected, and where the data will be collected. After individual goals are set for students, teams should check whether goals could be graphed by asking the following questions

- "Is the time frame defined?"
- "Are the measurement conditions clear?"
- "Is the behavior to be measured defined?"
- "Are the criteria for success designated?"

Case Example

Rich is a fourth-grade student who reads 70 WCPM in the fall. The target score for fall of grade 4 is 95 WCPM. After several attempted interventions and reviewing all data on Rich's reading performance, the GLT referred him to the PST, who decided that he would receive an specific individualized EBI for 30 minutes per day. The team also determined

TABLE 7.1. Growth Estimates Based on Research

	Screening/ benchmark	Intervention design	Monitor progress: Skill	Monitor progress: General
Emergent (typically grades K–1) Target: PA to decoding	MPS measures (alphabetic principle, PA)	Quick phonemic awareness (QPA)	DIBELS PSF (specific PA task—e.g., rhyming task)	DIBELS PSF
			1-minute assessment each week	1-minute assessment every other week
Beginning (typically grades 1–2, but could be 3) Target: decoding	MPS measures (ORF)	QPA, NWF, and WTW	DIBELS NWF (specific NWF—e.g., long vowel sounds)	FAIP ORF
			1-minute assessment each week	1-minute assessment every other week
Transitional (typically grades 2–3) Target: decoding to fluency	MPS measures (ORF and MAP)	MAP, ORF, and WTW	DIBELS NWF or DIBELS instructional-level ORF	FAIP ORF
			1-minute assessment each week	1-minute assessment every other week
Intermediate (typically grade 3) Target: Fluency to comprehension	MPS measures (ORF and MAP)	MAP, ORF, and WTW	DIBELS instructional-level ORF	FAIP ORF
			1-minute assessment each week	1-minute assessment every other week

Note. PA, phonemic awareness; NWF, nonsense-word fluency; LSF, letter-sound fluency; LNF, letter-naming fluency; PSF, phoneme segmentation fluency; WTW, words their way; ORF, oral reading fluency; FAIP, Formative Assessment for Instructional Planning.

TABLE 7.2 Growth Targets from Reading and Math from Fuchs et al. (2005) and the St. Croix River Education District

Grade level	Oral reading fluency		MAZE growth rate (Fuchs et al.)	Math digits correct growth rate (Fuchs et al.)
	Fuchs et al.	SCRED		
1	2 words per week	1.67 words per week	n/a	0.5 digits per week
2	2 words per week	1.52 words per week	0.84 items per week	0.5 digits per week
3	1.5 words per week	1.25 words per week	0.84 items per week	0.5 digits per week
4	1.1 words per week	1.03 words per week	0.84 items per week	1.15 digits per week
5	0.8 words per week	0.68 words per week	0.84 items per week	1.15 digits per week
6	0.65 words per week		0.84 items per week	1 digit per week

that his progress would be monitored twice per week using grade 4 AIMSweb passages. Mr. Huiskens, the school psychologist, will be responsible for collecting data every Tuesday and Thursday at 8:45 A.M. Rich's goal is as follows: By June 2012 (time frame), when presented with randomly selected fourth-grade AIMSweb probes (conditions), Rich will read (behavior) 127 WCPM (criterion for success).

EVALUATING INTERVENTION EFFECTS: MANAGING PROGRESS MONITORING DATA

Student progress monitoring data should be graphically displayed to aid in interpretation. Consider the following ORF progress monitoring data collected on a sixth-grade student: 62, 68, 61, 70, 69, 63, 56, 67, 71, 71, 76, 61, 84, 64, 76, 102, 95, 94, 114, 123, 91, 115, and 119. Is it easy to spot the trend? Do you know when different interventions have been tried? Now, examine the same data displayed on a graph (see Figure 7.1). How is this student progressing toward his goal? How many interventions have been tried?

As discussed in Chapter 5, student data are easily interpreted by examining progress monitoring graphs. When setting up individual progress monitoring graphs, the first step is to label and define the x- and y-axis. The x-axis typically is time (e.g., days, weeks, or months), and the y-axis is the behavior to be measured (e.g., number of WCPM, percent engaged). Second, each graph should have an aimline to compare student data. The aimline is drawn by connecting the median baseline data point to the final goal. Whenever an instructional change is made or an intervention is added, a vertical line should be drawn on the graph at the point on the x-axis when the change was made. Finally, remember not to connect data points across interventions! A sample graph with all essential elements is shown in Figure 7.2.

Schools will need to decide whether to use paper or electronic graphing systems. Electronic graphing systems are preferred, as they save time, reduce error, and may be easily shared with other team members. Both DIBELS and AIMSweb have features that will graphically display data and create many user-friendly reports. Districts pay a per-pupil fee to use these Internet-based systems. Graphs also may be created using Microsoft Excel, although this process is a bit more labor intensive than using an Internet-based system or a paper graph. Finally, there are free graphing tools available on the Internet (e.g., ChartDog at *www.interventioncentral.com*).

DECISION-MAKING RULES

Once progress monitoring data are collected, the data must be used to aid in instructional decision making. As a result, each building will need to determine the process for reviewing student data. We recommend that buildings set up regular data review meetings. Staff who participate in data reviews should use decision-making rules to judge the effectiveness of interventions. It is helpful for people interpreting graphs to be familiar with the concepts of

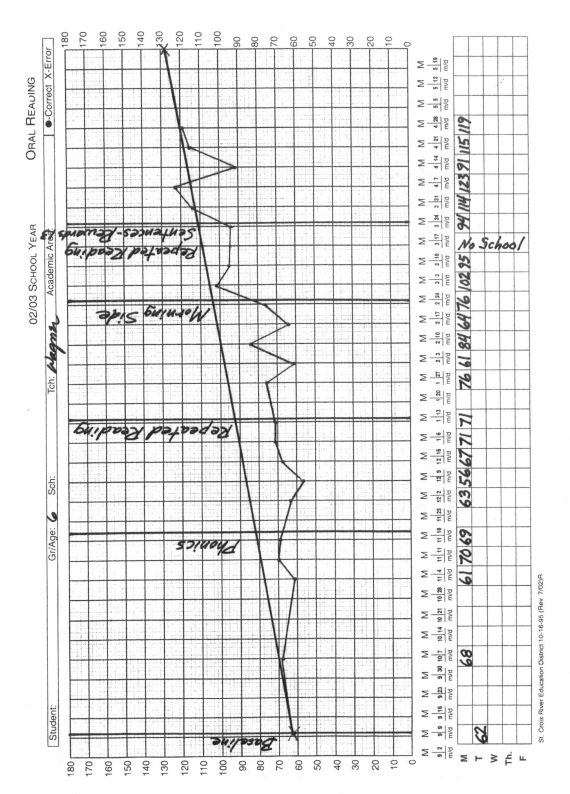

FIGURE 7.1. Progress monitoring graph.

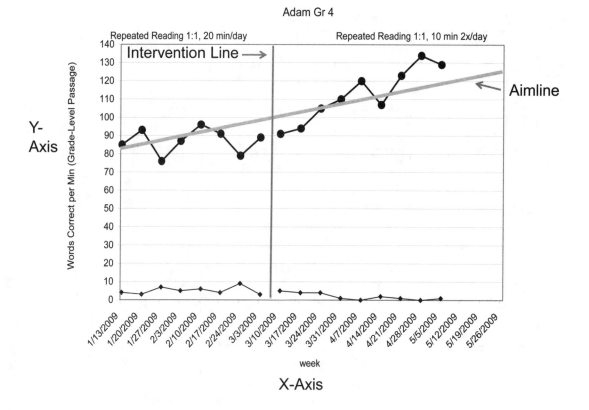

FIGURE 7.2. How to set up a graph.

level, slope, aimline, and trendline. Level refers to the student's current performance (e.g., 40 WCPM). Slope is the student's rate of improvement over time (e.g., 2.0 words per week gain). The aimline is the expected growth rate over time, and the trendline is the actual growth rate. Familiarity with these terms will aid in selecting an appropriate decision-making rule.

There are two decision-making methods for evaluating progress. The first method is the "consecutive data point" rule. Using this method, the student's data points are compared to the aimline. If three consecutive data points fall below the aimline, an instructional change is discussed. If three consecutive data points are above the aimline, the team considers fading the intervention or raising the goal. If three consecutive data points are consistent with the aimline, the current intervention is maintained. It is important to note that teams may decide to make different decisions than the rule. For example, a team may find that a student has three consecutive data points below the aimline, but they decide to continue the intervention due to an accelerated growth and other data sources. Thus the consecutive data point rule triggers the discussion, but many sources of data are used to guide decision making, including professional judgment. Many school districts use a three, four, or five consecutive data point rule. Although the empirical research does not dictate how many consecutive data points should be used for decision making, it is important to consider the progress monitoring schedule in place. If a five consecutive data point rule is used and data are collected monthly, then 5 months may pass before the team may consider an instructional change. As soon as a student begins to display flat rates of progress, the team should consider monitoring progress more frequently.

Although graphs are very useful tools, they may not be the best approach to make decisions. A second method to evaluate student progress is to calculate the rate of improvement (ROI) or slope using the ordinary least squares procedure. This procedure shows the general trend of the student's data. Although comparing individual student data to the aimline is a relatively easy process by which to interpret the data, measurement error can have a significant impact on the decisions that are made (Burns, Scholin, Kosciolek, & Livingston, 2010). Christ (2006) demonstrated that the measurement error associated with decisions made with fewer than eight to 10 data points are largely due to measurement error. In order to calculate a reliable slope, at least eight data points are needed. More recent research is indicating that as many as 12–15 data points are needed for a reliable slope (Christ, 2006).

Many of the commercial progress monitoring systems such as DIBELS and AIMSweb will calculate slope automatically, eliminating the need for school personnel to complete this step. However, both of these programs will calculate slope with as few as two data points. Thus, if these programs are used, school personnel must know not to have the programs calculate slope until the minimal number of data points are obtained (e.g., eight). If commercial programs are not used, slope can be calculated using Microsoft Excel.

Once a trendline is drawn through the data, comparisons can be made with the aimline to assist in instructional decisions. If the trendline is flatter than the goal line, instruction should be changed in order to accelerate progress. If the trendline is steeper than the goal line, either the goal should be raised or the intervention faded. If trendline is consistent with the goal line, the intervention should be maintained.

Both the consecutive data point rule and trendline–aimline comparison are ways for teams to evaluate student progress. However, both methods are general guidelines and should be used with other sources of data (e.g., classroom work, other test scores, student engagement) and professional judgment. Regardless of the interpretive system (e.g., consecutive data point rule vs. numeric slopes), a system needs to be established for recording data. Some schools we have worked with have one person in charge of entering data on the computer program or on the paper graph. In other instances, each person who collects progress monitoring data records and/or graphs student data. It is recommended that a building team meet annually to review the decision-making process and to identify any issues or concerns.

Dealing with Bounce

At times, teams will notice that progress monitoring data may be quite variable (i.e., bounce). When bounce occurs, teams should determine whether any measurement problem exists. Teams should explore whether the measures are being administered and scored with fidelity. A quick interrater reliability check can be done by having someone observe the person responsible for administering and scoring progress monitoring measures, noting whether correct administration and scoring procedures are being used. Teams should also determine whether the progress monitoring materials are of similar difficulty level. If passages are not of similar difficulty level, variable performance may be due to passages that are either too easy or too hard. Districts that use AIMSweb or DIBELS next can be assured that progress monitoring probes in the area of reading have been equated for standard difficulty level. Another measurement issue that may affect variability of performance is who administers probes, where, and when. For some students, these factors can influence performance.

When teams have ruled out measurement problems as a possible reason for variability, we recommend additional tips for teams that may help minimize bounce and aid in decision making. First, teams may consider looking at trend over a longer period of time. As mentioned earlier, a minimum of eight data points are necessary for obtaining reliable trend or growth estimates. Second, if only one progress monitoring passage is being used for progress monitoring, teams could administer three probes per session and graph the median score. Third, teams may increase the frequency of measurement if bounce is occurring. For example, if data are variable when data are collected twice per month, the frequency of progress monitoring could be bumped up to weekly. Finally, teams should be encouraged to look at all sources of data (e.g., errors, mastery data, and other tests) and look for converging evidence of progress or lack thereof.

RESPONDING TO INADEQUATE PROGRESS

One of the most frustrating experiences for teams is when, despite their best efforts, students do not make adequate progress. Many times, the first inclination is to refer the student for a special education evaluation. However, even if the student qualifies for special education, the team still needs to identify effective interventions. The goal in an RTI framework is to identify successful interventions, not qualifying students for special education services. Enhancing student progress depends on a systematic problem-solving process. When student progress is inadequate, teams need to revert to the problem-solving process and focus on problem analysis. The goal of problem analysis is to figure out why the problem is occurring. Teams typically develop hypotheses about why the problem is occurring based on current data. Sometimes, the wrong hypothesis is selected and teams need to collect additional data on student's skills to "replan" the intervention. Before embarking on a "redo" of problem analysis, teams should consider the following three questions:

> **The goal in an RTI framework is to identify successful interventions, not qualify students for special education services.**

1. *Is the intervention being implemented with fidelity?* Interventions that have been identified through empirical research as being effective should be implemented as they were designed. It important that interventionists receive training on the intervention and feedback on their performance. They should not deliver interventions until they have mastered the intervention in training sessions. The best way to check whether an intervention is

being implemented with fidelity is through direct observation. Many districts require that interventions be scripted, listing the essential steps of the intervention. These scripts may be turned into direct observation protocols. An example of a script and checklist is found in Figures 7.3 and 7.4.

2. *Is the intervention being delivered with the amount of time and intensity as planned?* Many times a team will select an appropriate intervention for a student, but the student does not receive the intended number of minutes per week of the intervention. For example, a team may determine that Isabella will receive a repeated reading intervention for 15 minutes per day, 5 days per week. Upon review of the intervention sessions, it is determined that Isabella receives the intervention for 7 minutes per session, three times per week. In this instance, the team may want to ensure that Isabella receives the desired number of intervention minutes per week before determining that the intervention is unsuccessful. It

---

DUET READING

Objective: To increase fluent reading particularly for students who
- often lose their spot while reading
- just don't get to the next word quickly enough
- benefit from a delayed model for correct word reading

Materials: Short texts that the student can read with *at least* 95% accuracy

Sequence:
1. **First reading**—Student reads the passage aloud. Teacher provides immediate standard error corrections. ("That word is _____. What word?" The student repeats the word. Teacher says, "Yes. That word is _____." Student goes back to the beginning of the sentence to begin again.)

2. **Second reading**—Teacher and student take turns reading EVERY OTHER WORD. Teacher first this time. Teacher should read with excellent expression to avoid typewriter-style output. Teacher should push the pace forward by reading each next word as soon as the student read the last word. Teacher provides standard error corrections immediately following any error. ("That word is _____. What word?" The student repeats the word. Teacher says, "Yes. That word is _____." Student goes back to the beginning of the sentence to begin again.)

3. **Third reading**—Teacher and student take turns reading EVERY OTHER WORD. Student first this time. Teacher continues to model excellent expression and to press the pace forward. Teacher provides standard error corrections immediately following any error. ("That word is _____. What word?" The student repeats the word. Teacher says, "Yes. That word is _____." Student goes back to the beginning of the sentence to begin again.)

4. **Fourth reading**—Student reads the entire passage out loud alone.

What If I Don't See Progress?
1. Does the student make no more than 5% errors on the text being utilized?
2. Have sessions been regular and frequent?
3. Has there been sufficient praise?
4. Are the error-correction procedures being delivered correctly and consistently?
5. Does the student have serious decoding issues that need to be addressed?

FIGURE 7.3. Sample intervention script.

DUET READING INTERVENTION INTEGRITY CHECKLIST		
Student Name: _____ Grade: _____ Date: _____		
Staff Name: _____ Observer: _____		
Intervention sequence	**Yes**	**No**
Teacher provides copy of text to student		
Reading 1: Student reads passage aloud and teacher provides standard error-correction procedure *immediately* after each student error.		
Reading 2: Teacher and student sit side by side, sharing the same passage.		
Teacher and student read, alternating each word. Teacher reads first word.		
Teacher reads with excellent expression.		
Teacher tracks with her/his finger under the words being read.		
Teacher presses the pace forward during reading.		
Teacher provides immediate error correction for each student error.		
Reading 3: Teacher and student read, alternating each word. Student reads first word.		
Teacher reads with excellent expression.		
Teacher tracks with her/his finger under the words being read.		
Teacher presses the pace forward during reading.		
Teacher provides immediate error correction for each student error.		
Reading 4: Student reads entire passage alone.		

FIGURE 7.4. Sample intervention checklist.

is important that the interventionist maintain accurate records of student attendance and participation.

3. *Is the student in the correct level of instructional materials?* This question focuses on whether a student's instructional level is known and that only materials appropriate for that level are being utilized in the intervention.

If the three questions above are answered satisfactorily, the team may determine additional areas to change within the intervention, including focus or skill, teaching strategies, materials, arrangements, time, and motivation. An instructional planning form (IPF) is a useful tool for documenting a student's current instructional plan and using it as the basis for discussing possible changes. A sample IPF is shown in Appendix 7.2. Using this form, grade-level or problem-solving team members work together to discuss the data, the student, and what intervention changes would have the best chance of success. Teams may decide that a student needs more instruction on a particular skill area (e.g., vocabulary, comprehension, phonics, fluency, math computation, math problem solving). They may determine that they are focusing on the correct skill, but the teaching strategies need to be changed to be more explicit, or include more modeling, more practice, or more previewing. Alternatively, a team may decide to modify the instructional materials so that they are easy and more appropriately matched to student interests. Another variable that can be changed is the arrangement, including group size, location, and teacher. Or teams may decide to change the amount of time the student receives the intervention (e.g., amount of time, days per week, time of day). Finally, teams may decide to modify an intervention to include more motivational strategies for the student. Many students who struggle have experienced years of failure and are not inherently excited to spend more time in subjects that are difficult for them. It is extremely important to build in systematic motivational programs to reward students for effort and participation in the intervention.

CONCLUSION

Making decisions about how individual students respond to EBIs is a cornerstone of the RTI framework. Without formative data on student progress, teachers have no way of knowing whether interventions are effective for individual students. Schools are under enormous pressure to ensure that all students make adequate progress toward becoming proficient in basic skill areas. To respond to this expectation, schools must have processes and procedures in place to (1) identify students in need of intervention, (2) set goals for students, (3) collect ongoing progress monitoring data on student achievement, and (4) evaluate student progress and identify appropriate instructional changes if necessary. This chapter provided information that will assist school staff in making decisions about individual students.

> Without formative data on student progress, teachers have no way of knowing whether interventions are effective for individual students.

Sample Bare-Bones Intervention Team Meeting Form

Meeting Date: _____

Student Name: _____   Teacher Name: _____

What is the problem behavior/academic concern? _____
_____

When does it happen? _____

How often does it happen? _____

What data (e.g., DBR, ODR) have been collected? If baseline data have been collected, please attach a graph.

_____

What is the logical reason for the child's engaging in the problem behavior/academic difficulty?

	Behavior problems	Academic problems
Acquisition	The student doesn't know how to do the right behavior.	The task is too hard for the student
Proficiency	Attention seeking/get something Escape something 　　Escape an academic task 　　Escape a social situation	The student has not had enough help doing the task (inaccurate). The student needs more practice (slow).
Generalization	The student has not had to do the behavior in this way before.	The student has not had to do the academic task this way before.

What EBIs would help with this problem? _____

Intervention plan details (attach an EBI brief if relevant)

1. _____
   _____
   _____

2. Who will do the intervention? _____

3. When will it be done? _____

4. How will the intervention be monitored? _____

When will a follow-up meeting be scheduled? _____

Problem-Solving Team Intervention Suggestions
A brief for each intervention can be found at *http://ebi.missouri.edu.*

Reason for behavior problem	Sample behavior interventions
Classwide	Good behavior game Response cost raffle
Acquisition	Say, show, check Sit and watch
Proficiency—gains something (e.g., attention)	Noncontingent reinforcement Behavior contracts Check-in check-out
Proficiency—escape	Choice-of-task sequence Antecedent modifications (individual or classwide) Instructional match (if academic escape)
Generalization	Incorporate functional mediators Reinforce natural occurrences

Reason for academic problem	Sample academic interventions
Acquisition	Cross-age peer tutoring Instructional match
Proficiency—accuracy	Cover, copy, compare Response cards
Proficiency—speed	Repeated readings Incremental rehearsal
Generalization	Incorporate functional mediators Reinforce natural occurrences

Adapted with permission from the Evidence Based Intervention Network (*http://ebi.missouri.edu*).

Sample Instructional Planning Form with Instructions

St. Croix River Education District
Chisago Lakes, East Central, Hinckley/
Finlayson, Pine City, and Rush City

PROBLEM-SOLVING TEAM
INSTRUCTIONAL PLANNING FORM

INSTRUCTIONAL PLANNING FORM

Student: _____   Grade: _____   School: _____

General Education Teacher: _____   Date: _____

Focus or skill	Activity		Materials	Arrangements	Time	Motivational strategies
	Teaching strategy					

122

INSTRUCTIONAL PLANNING FORM
INTERVIEW PROTOCOL

Purpose

The Instructional planning form (IPF) is used to record the activities that comprise a student's program of instruction (or any other academic subject). For each activity, you are asked to describe the typical materials, instructional arrangements, length of time, and motivational strategies that are involved.

Directions for the Interviewer

Before You Meet with the Teacher

1. Give the teacher a blank IPF, a completed example, and the description of the purpose of the IPF.
2. Set up a time to conduct the interview, preferably when the teacher is likely to be able to meet with you uninterrupted. The meeting should take about 20–25 minutes.
3. Tell the teacher that it is *not* necessary to complete the form in advance of your meeting.

When You Meet with the Teacher

BEFORE YOU BEGIN THE IPF INTERVIEW

1. Remind the teacher about the purpose of the IPF, how long the interview is likely to take, and how the information on the IPF will be used.
2. If the teacher has completed the IPF, use the completed form to guide the interview, that is, paraphrase or clarify each section of the completed form and make changes as needed.

DURING THE INTERVIEW

In general: Use the form to guide your questions. Fill out each section in front of the teacher, so he/she can see what you write. Keep your written responses brief (i.e., short phrases, not a long narrative). Ask for specifics: Who? What? How many? Paraphrase and clarify the teacher's description until you can record the critical features of each activity clearly.

1. Begin by asking about the main activities in reading.
2. Number the activities according to the typical sequence in which they occur.
3. For each activity in turn, complete a row on the form as follows:

ACTIVITY

Focus or Skill
- State the main focus or aspect of reading that the activity is designed to address (e.g., comprehension, decoding skills, fluency building, vocabulary).

Teaching Strategy
- Describe the general strategy that the teacher uses (e.g., round-robin reading, oral responses to oral questions from the teacher, reciprocal teaching, reading aloud with peer tutor).
- Include a description of a typical homework assignment.

Materials

- With textbooks, give the name, level, and title (e.g., Macmillan, Grade 5, Level 1, Landscapes; SRA Corrective Reading 2B).
- For other books or materials, describe the general type and give some examples (e.g., student's choice from books in class library, several books by Judy Blume).

Arrangements

- Who will run the activity (e.g., teacher, aide, peer tutor)?
- Estimate the number of students who will be involved and their general level of reading skills (e.g., entire class, 24; low reading group. 5 students; 3–4 students, mixed skills).

Time

- Estimate (within 5 minutes) the amount of time the student will engage in each activity on a typical day.
- If the time varies systematically from day to day, describe how (e.g., Monday: 15 minutes; Tuesday: 0; Wednesday–Friday: 10 minutes).

Motivational Strategies

- Describe what the teacher does to motivate the student during each activity (e.g., points for questions answered correctly; rocket chart of pages read; verbal praise).
- Ask the teacher an open-ended question about components of the student's reading program that may not have come up during the interview (e.g., "Is there anything else that you do to help [the student's] reading that we haven't talked about?"). Record this information on the IPF.

AFTER THE INTERVIEW

Thank the teacher for cooperating.

After You Meet with the Teacher

Get the teacher a copy of the completed IPF as soon as possible.

CHAPTER 8

Special Education Eligibility

At last, federal and state laws regarding the identification of students with learning disabilities (LD) is catching up to science. For years, research in the area of mild disabilities has denounced the practice of using IQ–achievement severe discrepancy models for determining whether students meet the criteria for a specific learning disability (SLD) (Aaron, 1997; Fletcher et al., 1998). We know that this type of an approach is a "wait-to-fail" model, as students typically do not exhibit large enough discrepancies to qualify for special education until after third grade. At the same time, research indicates that early intervention is critical for students with achievement problems (Brown-Chidsey, 2007). Others criticize IQ–achievement discrepancy approaches due to the lack of validity for the model, citing that current evidence does not exist showing that students who have a severe discrepancy between intelligence and achievement behave and can be treated in qualitatively different ways. Finally, others focus on the lack of treatment validity for IQ tests. When one considers the time and resources needed to administer and score intelligence tests, it becomes difficult to justify allocating resources to this activity when the tests do not contribute reliable information for planning, implementing, and evaluating instructional interventions (Aaron, 1997).

When the Individuals with Disabilities Education Improvement Act (IDEIA) was reauthorized in 2004, the federal government was aware of the criticisms of the IQ–achievement approach to SLD identification. Prior to IDEIA reauthorization, the President's Council on Excellence in Special Education was convened in 2001 to collect information and study issues related to federal, state, and local special education programs with the goal of recommending policies for improving the education performance of students with disabilities. In their report, they recommended eliminating IQ tests from the SLD identification process to shift the emphasis in special education away from determining whether students are eligible for services and toward providing students the interventions they need for academic success. They went on to report little justification for the ubiquitous use of IQ tests for children with high-incidence disabilities, except when intellectual disability is a consideration, especially given the cost and lack of evidence indicating that IQ test results are related meaningfully to intervention outcomes. Instead, they recommended implementing models during the identification and assessment process that are based on a student's RTI and that progress monitoring data from these processes be used to assess progress in children who receive special education services.

Thus, when IDEIA was reauthorized in 2004, language was included permitting alternative identification methods for SLD. Currently, state education agencies (SEAs) can no longer mandate that local education agencies (LEAs) use a severe discrepancy formula between intellectual ability and achievement in determining whether a student meets the criteria for SLD. Instead, SEAs must permit the use of a process that determines whether students respond to scientific, research-based interventions as part of the evaluation process. In addition, the SEA may permit the use of other alternative research-based procedures for determining whether a child is eligible for special education under the category of SLD.

ADVANTAGES OF
A RESPONSE-TO-INTERVENTION APPROACH TO ELIGIBILITY

Several advantages become apparent when using data from the RTI process to aid in entitlement decisions. First, while the IQ–achievement model is criticized for being a "wait-to-fail" model, using data from the RTI framework eliminates the need for students to fail before receiving help. Schools that implement an RTI framework operate under a preventive model in which students are identified early and receive interventions and supports based on their needs. Second, lack of appropriate instruction is ruled out as the cause for a student's poor academic performance, ensuring that a student would not be labeled as SLD due to inadequate instruction. Third, assessment approaches within an RTI framework are directly used to inform intervention. As a result, school psychologists are able to use their assessment time to focus on functional assessment activities rather than on assessment activities that contribute little information to intervention planning. Engaging in these types of functional assessment activities helps shift the emphasis away from special education eligibility and toward getting students the instruction they need to succeed. Finally, this approach emphasizes providing services to students based on need (as opposed to labels) in the least restrictive environment.

> **Engaging in these types of functional assessment activities helps shift the emphasis away from special education eligibility and toward getting students the instruction they need to succeed.**

This chapter focuses on the process for making eligibility determinations in the category of SLD using an RTI approach. First, the essential components needed for decision making are outlined. Second, we discuss common criticisms of using alternative models for SLD identification and our response to these criticisms. Next, we address common implementation concerns, including documentation of the process, definition of rigorous interventions, timelines, and the definition of a full evaluation. Finally, a case study is used to provide an example of how data from the RTI framework can be used to assist in special education entitlement decisions.

USING DATA FROM THE RESPONSE-TO-INTERVENTION FRAMEWORK FOR MAKING ENTITLEMENT DECISIONS

Essential Conditions to Support a Response-to-Intervention Process

The term RTI is commonly used in a broad sense to refer to a multi-tiered service delivery system that does not make sharp distinctions between disabled and nondisabled students, rather than a separate procedure for determining whether a student has an LD (Tilly et al., 2005). Within the multi-tiered system, emphasis is placed on high-quality core instruction for all students, supplemental instruction for some students, and intensive instruction for a few students. Assessments occur at all levels, beginning with universal screening for all students three times per year and more frequent progress monitoring for students with achievement difficulties. Interventions across the tiers are informed by direct measures of instructionally relevant data, and student progress is measured frequently during interventions. Teams do not consider referring students for a special education evaluation until interventions at Tiers 2 and 3 have proven ineffective. School teams typically begin by implementing a standard treatment protocol (STP) intervention with a small group of students. Students who do not make progress in an STP intervention receive a more intensive, individualized intervention carefully tailored to their needs. If a student makes significant rapid progress during an intervention, it is possible that the academic deficit was due to prior lack of appropriate instruction or environmental challenges, rather than a disability inherent in the student (Gresham, 2002; Lyon et al., 2001). An insufficient RTI alerts teams that a student may need increasingly intensive levels of service and signaling the need for special education services. This lack of responsiveness to general education interventions constitutes a significant part of the data that is reviewed when a referral for special education is made. However, when interpreting a student's rate of progress, teams should be cautioned against denying eligibility based on noticeable improvement or increased growth rate. Rather, teams need to determine whether the increased growth rate is due to an intensive intervention that meets the definition of specialized instruction and is unlikely to be sustained with regular education resources.

Because entitlement decisions are based in large part on interventions delivered in regular education settings, it is critical that schools have a solid RTI framework in place *before* using data from a student's participation in interventions to make entitlement decisions. Table 8.1 describes the essential conditions to support an effective RTI framework.

TABLE 8.1. Essential Conditions to Support an RTI Process for Entitlement

- District-level and school-level leadership and support.
- Job-embedded professional development on the RTI framework.
- High-quality core curricula in academic and social behavior areas implemented with well-defined scope and sequence plans across grades.
- A multi-tiered system of scientifically validated interventions appropriately matched to student needs is established and supported through the master schedule.
- Clearly articulated local assessment plan that includes screening procedures for all students at least three times per year; diagnostic assessment as needed; a plan for progress monitoring those at risk; and outcomes evaluation at least annually.
- Systematic use of data to monitor the effectiveness of core, supplemental, and intensive instruction.
- Grade-level teams established for staff collaboration around student data.
- Building-based problem-solving teams with balanced representation from all general and specialized teaching groups.
- Direct observation of intervention fidelity.
- Documentation procedures to track students' status and monitor interventions.

Criteria for Eligibility under a Response-to-Intervention Framework

Each state ultimately promulgates their own rules regarding special education entitlement using data from the RTI framework. While variations among states are certain to exist, five broad areas are typically included in the eligibility decision-making process.

1. A "dual discrepancy" (DD) exists where the student's *level of academic performance* and *rate of growth* is significantly discrepant from grade-level expectations.
2. Empirically validated interventions are used and documented with the student in a multi-tiered service delivery model.
3. Documentation exists that the interventions are delivered with integrity and with the amount of time and intensity planned.
4. Psychometrically sound progress monitoring measures are used.
5. Exclusionary factors are addressed.

Each of these criteria are discussed in more detail in the next section.

Dual Discrepancy

In order for students to qualify for special education services using data from the RTI framework, they must exhibit low academic achievement relative to grade-level standards and make insufficient progress over time. For example, if a student's level of reading performance as measured by oral reading fluency (ORF) is below a particular criterion (e.g., 10th percentile) and his or her rate of growth is insufficient compared to expected growth rates for their grade level, then that student would meet the DD criterion. Several studies exist that suggest that DD data significantly differentiate reading skills of children at risk for reading failure with and without a DD profile (Burns & Senesac, 2005; Speece & Case, 2001; Speece, Case, & Molloy, 2003). Each state defines what measures can be used to determine a dual discrepancy. For determining discrepancy on level of achievement, general outcome measures and/or individually administered achievement tests are commonly used. States also dictate whether local, state, or national normative groups are used to determine a discrepancy in level of achievement. However, most proponents of an RTI framework would argue for the use of local norms in decision making because they are theoretically more representative of the milieu in which the student is currently functioning. Students are compared to other students receiving the same instruction coming from similar backgrounds and learning experiences. Mild handicaps are often described as situational, and judgments of "significant difference" are determined by the local social contexts within which a student's behavior occurs.

When determining inadequate rate of progress, psychometrically sound and sensitive measures of achievement should be used. Most districts use a member of the curriculum-based measurement (CBM) family of instruments (e.g., AIMSweb, DIBELS, Easy CBM). Determining inadequate rate of academic progress can be problematic when making comparisons to local expectations. School districts typically screen students three times per year using CBMs. If a district wanted to compare a student's rate of growth to other students in that same grade, they would need to monitor *all* students on a regular basis to make that comparison. Due to limited resources, it really isn't practical for districts to monitor all students' progress. And, one could argue, it isn't necessary to monitor students who are at or above grade-level expectations more than three times per year. Although the empirical research literature does contain examples of growth rates at various grade levels, these growth rates are based on national normative samples that may not apply to an individual district's demographics. An alternative is to use criterion-referenced target scores (discussed in Chapter 7) and determine the amount of growth needed at each grade level to reach the spring target. Districts can set a confidence interval around each grade-level growth rate and compare a student's growth rate to the expected rate for that grade level.

Documentation of Empirically Validated Interventions

Federal law specifies that states must allow districts to use a process that determines whether students respond to scientific, research-based interventions as part of the evaluation process. Thus districts must be knowledgeable consumers of research and use interventions that have substantial evidence of effectiveness through multiple outcome evaluations. In addition, districts must have a tiered system of intervention supports available within the building. Most districts use a problem-solving model of decision making for individualizing interventions for students. It is critical to have a documentation system in place to evaluate whether this model has been followed with integrity. Form 8.1 at the end of the chapter displays the essential steps to develop, implement, and evaluate interventions using a problem-solving model.

Documentation of Treatment Integrity

Treatment integrity is the degree to which a planned intervention is implemented as designed (Moncher & Prinz, 1991). Without checking on implementation integrity, teams cannot be sure that interventions are being applied as designed (DuPaul & Stoner, 2003). If the intervention is not applied as designed, progress (or lack thereof) cannot be attributed to the specific plan (Kaufman & Flicek, 1995). Evaluation of treatment integrity is imperative when making entitlement decisions to avoid making erroneous decisions about the reasons for low achievement and inadequate progress. A few states have defined treatment integrity in their state rules (Zirkel & Thomas, 2010). For example, the Wisconsin SLD rule states that the intervention must be applied in a manner highly consistent with its design,

> **Evaluation of treatment integrity is imperative when making entitlement decisions to avoid making erroneous decisions about the reasons for low achievement and inadequate progress.**

and be provided to the pupil at least 80% of the recommended number of weeks, sessions, and minutes per session. The implication for districts using data from the RTI framework to make entitlement decisions is that they must have a system to check on fidelity of implementation and a documentation system to track intervention logistics.

Reliable and Valid Progress Monitoring Measures

Federal rule states that data-based documentation of repeated assessments of achievement at reasonable intervals reflecting formal assessment of student progress during instruction must be provided to the child's parents. When evaluating a student's rate of progress during an intervention, districts must use progress monitoring measures that are valid, reliable, brief, easy to administer, and sensitive to growth over short periods of time. Most tools that meet these requirements are members of the curriculum-based measurement (CBM) family. Some state rules have specified that the measures used must have multiple equal or nearly equal forms to eliminate variability in data. The National Center for Progress Monitoring (*www.studentprogress.org*) is a valuable resource for reviewing available progress monitoring tools. The more recent National Center for Intensive Interventions (*www. intensiveintervention.org*) will soon provide a vetted rating of behavior measures that use evidence to support their use for behavioral progress monitoring.

Exclusionary Factors

Federal and state SLD definitions continue to require exclusion of other factors in determining entitlement for special education services. Teams must document that a child's underachievement is not due to lack of appropriate instruction. In addition, they must demonstrate that the child's underachievement and insufficient progress are not primarily the result of (1) a visual, hearing, or motor disability; (2) intellectual disability; (3) emotional disturbance; (4) cultural factors; (5) environmental or economic disadvantage; or (6) limited English proficiency.

CRITICISMS OF THE RESPONSE-TO-INTERVENTION APPROACH TO ENTITLEMENT

Limited Research to Scale

Many critics of an RTI framework argue that there is limited research on "scaling up" the framework to practice. However, moving from policy to implementation is always a challenge any time new practices are brought to scale. There is no doubt that districts will need technical assistance on intervention development and progress monitoring procedures. However, research does exist in the area of academic and behavioral interventions that include RTI as a component (Heartland Area Education Agency, 2004; Kovaleski, Gickling, & Morrow, 1998; Marston, Muyskens, Lau, & Canter, 2003; McNamara & Hollinger, 2003). Descriptions of many large-scale implementation efforts are available in the literature (Jimerson, Burns, & VanDerHeyden, 2007), and four consensus reports at the national level have concluded that the RTI research base is sound. Thus there is consensus that the evidence is sufficient to justify large-scale implementation of RTI at this time (Bradley, Danielson, & Hallahan, 2002; Donovan & Cross, 2002; Finn, Rotherham, & Hokansen, 2001; President's Commission on Excellence in Special Education, 2001).

Identification of True Learning Disabilities

While there is clear consensus among LD researchers to abandon the ability–achievement discrepancy model, many people are concerned that using an RTI framework for entitlement decisions will not identify students with true learning disabilities and that the fundamental concept of LD is changed. Two of the fundamental concepts around LD were the notion of an "unexpected discrepancy" in achievement. Within an RTI framework, the concepts of "discrepancy" and "unexpected" are still retained. However, instead of defining these concepts based on IQ tests, they are gauged in relation to the effectiveness of carefully targeted interventions. We expect students with academic skill deficits to respond to scientific, research-based interventions that are matched to student's needs and delivered with fidelity and intensity. In addition, it is important to note that other components such as low achievement, exclusion, and RTI are already part of most definitions and would remain intact.

Overidentification

A common fear about using data from the RtI framework to make entitlement decisions is that the "floodgates" will open and overidentification of students with disabilities will occur. Yet data from other states and districts using an RTI approach do not indicate that students are overidentified as LD. In fact, meta-analytic research found that districts that use an RTI framework identify fewer than 2% of the students as SLD, compared to a national average of about 5% (Burns et al., 2005). Furthermore, the St. Croix River Education District has been using data from the RTI process to make special education entitlement decisions since 2005, and they have shown a 50% reduction in the number of students identified as LD. At the same time, major gains in achievement for all students have been demonstrated. It is important to note that most entitlement frameworks require a dual discrepancy in both level of achievement and rate of improvement, so it is erroneous to think that any student with low achievement will qualify for special education under this model. Rather, students who are the most discrepant in their level of achievement *and* who make minimal growth will be considered for special education services.

Use of Local Norms for Decision Making

Another common criticism around an RTI approach for SLD identification centers on the issue of whether it is fair to identify students as SLD based on local norms. Many researchers and practitioners argue that students will be SLD in one district and not qualify in another district. While this is true, the current system also suffers from this same flaw. Deterring eligibility for special education services has always centered around two questions: (1) Does the student meet the eligibility criteria for a disability? and (2) Does the student have significant educational needs? In an RTI framework, schools provide special education services to the students who are the most discrepant from local expectations and have the most intensive instructional needs. Depending on district demographics, there may be students in one district who have instructional needs in one district but not another.

COMMON IMPLEMENTATION CONCERNS

Documentation of Response to Intervention

A popular implementation question centers on when districts are required to document student participation in interventions. We suggest that documentation start when the student receives supplemental interventions and support (Tier 2). If the student is eventually referred for a special education evaluation, then the mandated timeline starts when the parent gives consent for an evaluation. The U.S. Department of Education has been quite clear that schools cannot delay a special education evaluation to complete an RTI process. In most cases, districts already have existing data that may be used to make entitlement decisions. The school personnel should be able to respond to an evaluation request by examining existing data to determine whether (1) more data are needed, (2) the referral is warranted, or (3) a learning disability is suspected. Although schools are obligated to respond to parent requests for evaluation, they can determine what the evaluation will consist of. Often, school staff can look at progress monitoring data within Tier 2 or 3 and conclude that those data are sufficient to rule out a disability.

Advocates for an RTI approach suggest that it will be a way for students to receive assistance more quickly than through traditional approaches, but skeptics quickly point out that to go from Tier 1 through Tiers 2 and 3 and into special education may require 8 to 16 weeks, which is a much longer time frame than allowed for a traditional special education evaluation. However, anyone who makes that argument likely does not understand RTI, or special education for that matter. The provision of interventions as students' progress through the tiers is an intervention model, not the assessment. The three-tiered model will not begin when the student is referred for a special education eligibility evaluation, but will already be in place as a schoolwide intervention approach, and the multidisciplinary evaluation team can simply examine existing data. We suggest also administering one standardized norm-referenced measure in the relevant academic domain in addition to examining RTI data, which could easily meet local, state, and federal mandates for eligibility consideration timelines.

Defining the Intensity of Interventions

School teams often struggle when determining whether interventions are intensive enough. Two factors should be considered when determining whether an intervention is highly intensive. First, the team should consider the amount of time allocated to the intervention. Most intense interventions usually are delivered at least 4 to 5 days per week for enough time to complete the intervention program. Second, interventions must be empirically validated and scientifically based. If the amount of time allocated to the intervention is insufficient and the intervention is not supported through empirical research, then the team needs to discuss why they think the intervention is "intense." Recent meta-analytic research has identified five components of an effective academic intervention resulting in significant achievement gains: (1) correctly targeted, (2) explicit teaching of the skill, (3) high repetition and frequent opportunities to respond, (4) appropriate instructional match (not too hard and not too easy), and (5) immediate corrective feedback (Burns, VanDerHeyden, & Boice, 2008). Thus school teams could examine potential interventions to determine whether those five elements are included. If not, then teams should be skeptical about the intensity of the intervention.

Definition of a "Full Evaluation"

Given the shift from a within-child discrepancy model to a more needs-based framework, it is not surprising that concerns and confusion exist about what constitutes a full evaluation. Many assert that teams are required to assess cognitive processing through individually administered tests of intelligence. IDEIA (2004) requires "a full and individual initial evaluation" prior to providing special education services (Pub. L. No 108–466 § 614 [a][1] [A]). Moreover, children with suspected disabilities must be assessed "in all areas related to the suspected disability" (§ 614 [b][3][B]). Thus the right to a comprehensive evaluation is again protected in special education law, but what is meant by the word *comprehensive*? It is important to note that there is no mandate for anything in the comprehensive evaluation, and there is no support for cognitive processing requirements in the preamble. In fact, the preamble states that "the Department does not believe that an assessment of psychological or cognitive processing should be required in determining whether a child has an SLD. There is no current evidence that such assessments are necessary or sufficient for identifying SLD. Furthermore, in many cases, these assessments have not been used to make appropriate intervention decisions" (p. 649 of final regulations).

It hardly seems possible that conducting one measure of intelligence and standardized measures of achievement could be more comprehensive than collecting data directly related to the problem for a period of weeks to measure the success of attempted interventions. Thus a comprehensive evaluation could include screening child characteristics that might affect achievement (vision, hearing, etc.) along with direct assessment of current skills, instructional environments, and behaviors. In instances where the RTI data do not provide all the information needed for eligibility determination and classification, then additional relevant data are collected as needed.

> **In instances where the RTI data do not provide all the information needed for eligibility determination and classification, additional relevant data are collected as needed.**

CASE STUDY

Billy is an eighth-grade student whose reading performance is well below grade-level expectations. As a result, he is having great difficulty in his content-area courses. His school has implemented an RTI framework for the past 5 years. Universal screening is conducted three times per year for all students, and tiered system of interventions and support has been established. GLTs meet monthly to review data on students and assist in designing standard treatment protocol interventions at Tier 2. The building PST meets weekly to individualize interventions for students who do not respond to Tier 2 interventions. The PST met to discuss how best to address Billy's need. They followed a systematic problem-solving model for decision making, including problem identification, problem analysis, plan development, plan implementation, and plan evaluation.

Intervention 1

Problem Identification

To identify the problem, a member of the team reviewed existing information on Billy's academic performance; interviewed teachers, parents, and Billy; conducted systematic observations of Billy in his classes; and examined testing information that was available. Following this process, they developed the following discrepancy statement: Billy is reading 52 WCPM with two errors on eighth-grade-level reading passages. The target for eighth-grade students in the spring is 170 WCPM.

Problem Analysis

Data from a variety of sources across the domains of instruction, curriculum, environment, and learner were collected to consider multiple hypotheses for the cause of the discrepancy. Converging data supported the hypothesis that Billy is discrepant from grade-level expectations because he needs additional practice to increase his reading fluency.

Plan Development

The team set a goal that, by May 2013, Billy will read 113 WCPM, with no errors, from grade 8 R-CBM passages. The rate of improvement should be 1.2 words correct per week. The instructional plan identified that Billy would participate in a small-group intervention using the *Six-Minute Solution* (e.g., repeated reading) for 15 minutes per day. Billy's progress was monitored using grade 8 AIMSweb reading passages on a weekly basis by the interventionist.

Plan Implementation

The school psychologist observed the teacher implementing the Six-Minute Solution. A script was used for training the teacher, and this same script was used during the observation. The observation indicated that the intervention was implemented correctly. In addition, the team verified that Billy was participating in the intervention on a daily basis for the appropriate amount of time and that data were collected and graphed as stated in the plan.

Plan Evaluation

The team examined Billy's progress monitoring graph and found that Billy's level of performance had not changed with the intervention and his rate of improvement was insufficient. Thus the team cycled through the problem-solving steps again to identify a more intensive intervention.

Intervention 2

The team confirmed that Billy is reading 58 WCPM with 2 errors on eighth-grade-level reading passages. The target for grade 8 is 170 WCPM with an expected growth rate of 1.2 words per week. They hypothesized that Billy needed more time in teacher-directed instruction with systematic modeling and error correction. They determined that Billy would receive small-group reading instruction daily for 50 minutes using the *Corrective Reading, Level B* curriculum. Progress would continue to be monitored on a weekly basis, and the goal remained the same. Direct observations confirmed the intervention was being delivered correctly. After 7 weeks of intervention, the team reviewed Billy's progress monitoring data (see Figure 8.1). Billy's level of performance did not change, and his rate of improvement was –0.4 words per week. The team decided to refer Billy to the student support team for a special education evaluation.

Entitlement Decision

After receiving consent for a special education evaluation, the team reviewed existing information and collected additional information through interviewing, observation, and testing. Billy's rate of improvement during the last intervention was –0.4 words per week. The mini-

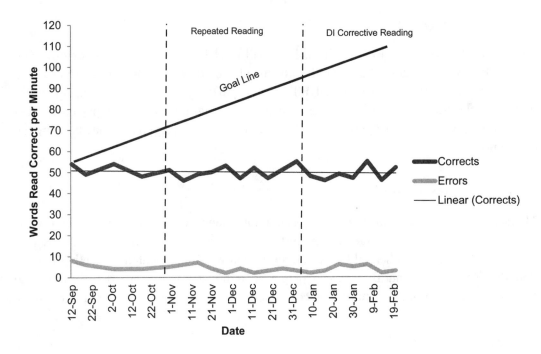

FIGURE 8.1. Progress monitoring data for the case of Billy.

mum expected growth rate for grade 8 was 0.28. Billy's level of performance was 52 WCPM on grade 8 reading passages. This level of performance corresponded to the 5th percentile. The team concluded that Billy had a dual discrepancy in his level of performance and rate of improvement compared to grade-level expectations. The team verified that the problem-solving process was used with fidelity to develop, implement, and evaluate interventions. The team verified a high degree of instructional need that must be addressed through special education services. In addition, the team addressed the exclusionary factors required by state law. They concluded that Billy was eligible for special education services under the category of SLD. However, it is important to note that an effective intervention was not identified at the point of special education entitlement. It is imperative that teams continue to analyze the problem, develop different hypotheses for why the problem is occurring, and modify the intervention until a positive growth trajectory is established. Districts should have an accountability mechanism in place to review data for special education students to verify that measurable goals are written, data are graphically displayed, decision-making rules are used to evaluate progress, and interventions are implemented when progress is insufficient.

CONCLUSION

Although a single method for identifying students with SLD has not emerged as superior, it is clear that the ability–achievement discrepancy approach is inadequate. Critics of an RTI approach state that attempts to broadly expand RTI models are uneven and not uniformly effective. However, in his testimony to Congress, Carnine (2003) stated "that is a problem with adult learning, not with the research on how children learn. The real issue centers around large-scale implementation, not on more research on how to implement RTI models or whether they are effective. Clearly, all the best intentions and new designs for improving the identification process and delivery of scientifically based interventions will fall short if the professional educators, administrators, and related and support personnel responsible for implementing these designs do not have the knowledge, skill, will, or resources to implement and sustain them. Formal training and ongoing technical assistance and support will be necessary for classroom teachers and related service providers to perform these tasks with fidelity and to use performance data in ways that inform classroom instruction" (D. Carnine, Testimony before Congress, March 2003).

FORM 8.1

Case Review
Protocol for Evaluating Integrity of the Problem-Solving Model

Problem-Solving Step	Intervention 1	Intervention 2
Problem Identification		
An initial discrepancy was defined in observable, measurable terms and quantified.		
Documented data from at least two sources converge to support the discrepancy statement.		
Student baseline data in the area of concern is collected and includes a minimum of three data points with standardized procedures for assessment. Baseline data are graphed.		
Problem Analysis		
Data from a variety of sources and domains were collected to consider multiple hypotheses for the cause of the identified discrepancy.		
A single hypothesis for the cause of the discrepancy was selected. At least two pieces of data converge to support this hypothesis. At least one of these is quantitative.		
Plan Development		
A data-based goal was established that describes the learner, conditions, expected performance, and a goal date. The goal is indicated on a graph.		
The intervention selected meets federal definition of scientifically research-based intervention. The selected intervention directly addresses the specific identified problem and the hypothesis for the cause of the discrepancy.		
A written intervention plan was clearly defined that explicitly describes what will be done, where, when, how often, how long, by whom, and with what resources.		
A written description of the progress monitoring plan was completed and includes who will collect data, data collection methods, conditions, and schedule.		

(continued)

From T. Chris Riley-Tillman, Matthew K. Burns, and Kimberly Gibbons (2013). Copyright by The Guilford Press. Permission to photocopy this form is granted to purchasers of this book for personal use only (see copyright page for details). Purchasers can download additional copies of this form from *www.guilford.com/riley-forms*.

Problem-Solving Step	Intervention 1	Intervention 2
A decision making rule was selected for use.		
A plan evaluation meeting was set for no more than 8 weeks after the plan is established.		
Plan Implementation		
A direct observation of the intervention was completed at least one time. Any discrepancies between the written plan and the intervention in action were noted and resolved. Observations continued until the intervention being delivered and the written intervention plan matched.		
Team documented agreement that the plan was carried out as intended.		
Team documented agreement that the student participated in the intervention as planned.		
Plan Evaluation		
Data were collected and graphed as stated in plan. The required number of data points were collected under the same intervention conditions after integrity was established.		
Team accurately determined and documented the level of student response to intervention on the plan evaluation form.		
Team decided to continue the plan unmodified, develop a modified plan, fade, or terminate the plan. Team documented this decision.		

CHAPTER 9

Conclusion

BACKDROP OF THE *RTI APPLICATIONS* VOLUMES

The idea behind the two *RTI Applications* volumes was born out of conversations between the first and second authors in 2009. At that time it was clear that RTI was quickly becoming a model that would be used across the United States as a preferred method of service delivery. While we were excited about the groundswell of RTI use, we also discussed our concerns about some missing pieces. These concerns bore out of a mix of work with schools implementing RTI and our related scholarship. Those concerns loosely fit in two areas. First, there seemed to be a lack of practitioner-oriented materials focusing on some of the more complicated elements of RTI. While there were superb books that provided a foundation for RTI use (e.g., *Response to Intervention, Second Edition: Principles and Strategies for Effective Practice* by Brown-Chisdey & Steege, 2010, and *Implementing Response-to-Intervention in Elementary and Secondary Schools, Second Edition* by Burns & Gibbons, 2012), there did not seem to be follow-up material that then expanded educational professionals' understanding of the core elements of RTI. There are some excellent in-depth academic treatments like the *Handbook of RTI* by Jimerson and colleagues (2007), but these writings were oriented more toward scholarly outlets than educational professionals. In reality, RTI in both theory and practice can be very complex and technical, and it was our opinion that for RTI to fulfill its vast potential for helping children in need, educational professionals should have a detailed understanding of RTI. Our second concern was that there are still many unknowns with RTI. We are happy to say that in just the last 4 years there have been significant advancements in intervention, assessment, design, analysis and decision making. Despite these advancements, there is still much work to be done. In our work with schools, there is often frustration about core RTI elements remaining undefined or core RTI tools not seeming to exist. We hope that these books will help define areas in which there remains necessary work to be done, as well as provide some guidance to schools about what to do when the right tool does not exist.

Moving forward, we fully understand that RTI is a dynamic model that is changing technically and practically while at the same time educational policy is shifting. This landscape of change must leave educational professionals considering how best to go about a professional development model for themselves as individuals, and for whole schools and districts. Rather than a static conclusion, we would like to conclude the *RTI Applications* books with a suggested professional development plan for those interested in implementing an RTI model in their school.

DISTRICTWIDE RESPONSE-TO-INTERVENTION PROFESSIONAL DEVELOPMENT PLAN

Our professional development model starts with a two-tiered approach to training. It is neither essential nor reasonable that everyone in each school will understand all elements of RTI. Rather, there is a basic level of understanding that all staff must obtain, and then more advanced knowledge that can reside with a smaller group. We borrow this approach from a number of sources, but in particular look at the widespread success of positive behavior interventions and supports (PBIS). PBIS uses a highly trained core team that then trains the rest of the school. In that model, the core team is responsible for both the initial school training (with support from the PBIS technical center) and then yearly retraining so that both the team, and then to a lesser extent the school as whole, can be up to date on current best practices in PBIS.

> **It is not essential that everyone in each school will understand all elements of RTI. There is a basic level of understanding that all staff must obtain, and then more advanced knowledge that can reside with a smaller group.**

It is important to note that there are a number of teams in a districtwide RTI model. In a single building, there are ideally three types of teams: a building team, a problem-solving team (PST), and grade-level teams (GLTs). Smaller, rural school districts may consider combining the PST and building teams. The building leadership team serves as the overarching management group for facilitating and evaluating implementation in a particular school. The building leadership teams help identify current assessment and intervention practices and skill sets needed for training through a comprehensive needs assessment process. In addition, they assist in building consensus and commitment. The primary roles of these teams include evaluating school achievement and behavior data to identify needed changes in existing tools, training and support, especially around fidelity of implementation. The main task of the PST is to support interventions for more intensive cases. This team will need the most in-depth knowledge with regard to intervention selection/implementation, assessment, design/analysis, and decision making using a systematic problem-solving model. Finally, GLTs are tasked with reviewing data from their grade level to evaluate core instruction, setting goals for the desired level of proficiency at their grade level, identifying students who are in need of supplemental instruction, and evaluating the effects of these interventions. Well-trained GLTs should also make decisions about Tier 2 resources and interventions. While those teams don't need the in-depth training of the core RTI teams, they do need a depth and breadth of understanding about the general model and relevant technical applications. For example, GLTs need to be trained to support Tier 2 services, which requires a great deal of intervention, assessment, and decision making.

In addition to these building teams, there should be a district RTI leadership team. The district leadership team has many responsibilities, including formulating an action plan, explaining how other district initiatives fit within the RtI framework, setting standards for fidelity of implementation, helping buildings conduct a self-study of existing practices, and encouraging buildings to abandon ineffective practices (planned abandonment). The district leadership team also formulates a plan for how to communicate the district action plan to key stakeholders across the district. The overall mission of the district RTI leadership team is to support RTI development in each school and ensure consistent practices district-wide. District and building leadership teams have somewhat similar roles, but on a different scale. Both assist in assessing district and building needs, providing leadership, building commitment, giving permission to change practices, and allocating resources to support change. Smaller, rural school districts may consider having one combined district/school leadership team, but larger districts should have both teams. In the absence of a district team, it is likely that each school will develop RTI procedures and instruments in a unique manner. Such variance across a district can cause some significant headaches. Considering the charge of each team, both should have an understanding of advanced RTI applications. With this basis they can train teams as well as develop policies that are consistent with best practices in RTI.

In terms of a district professional development plan, we offer the following suggestions. (See Appendix 9.1 for an example of a district RTI training plan developed by the third author for the state of Minnesota.) While elements of this plan will likely need to be altered for a specific district, this plan outlines core elements necessary in successfully developing a districtwide RTI system.

Train All Core Response-to-Intervention Teams in the Advanced Applications of Response to Intervention

The task of training the district, building, and problem-solving teams to become the experts in RTI for a district or school is a significant endeavor. Between the philosophy, all of the critical details, and the challenges of mounting a districtwide/schoolwide plan, there is a tremendous amount of training for core team members. To make this task a bit more palatable we suggest breaking it into two steps. First, teams need to take time to learn the general concept of RTI. Although it may be tempting to rush through this step and get to the gritty details, this urge should be resisted. In our experience districts often are "engaged" in RTI, but don't fully comprehend the model. Specifically, we see schools collect formative data yet not use that data to drive decisions. Unfortunately, efficiently collecting CBM data does not constitute RTI, and in fact can frustrate school staff who spend time collecting data for no apparent use. In contrast, schools that take a year to simply allow team members to become local experts then have individuals who can make sure that such mistakes are not made. RTI is both a dynamic process and cluster of technical skills, and the dynamic process supports the use of the specific skills to actually help children. To learn this process, team members should visit other schools or districts that are seasoned in implementing RTI, have RTI experts visit their district/school to provide support, attend workshops/ trainings, and have book studies using materials that provide a solid base of RTI expertise.

Once the teams have an understanding of RTI theory, team members should focus on each core area of intervention, assessment, design and analysis, problem solving, schoolwide organization, and "other." The purpose of RTI applications was to provide such a foundation in relation to intervention, assessment, design, analysis, and decision making. We add the ubiquitous "other" category, as there are many areas of study that can be useful for RTI schools. We applaud teams who seek out unique related training experiences, but we do suggest that those be pursued after core training is accomplished.

Train All Educational Professionals Involved in the Basics of Response to Intervention

After core teams have an in-depth understating of the RTI model, they should go about training the whole school. This is the particular task of the building RTI team, with support from the district RTI team and the school PST. The goal of the whole-school training is not to have every teacher fully comprehend a multiple baseline design, but rather to have a deep understanding of what they will be responsible for and a more general understanding of how that fits into the larger process. This step is critical if we expect GLTs to accomplish their role in RTI. Teachers must be trained to implement EBI, use formative assessment methods, and participate on teams to review that data and make decisions. In addition, teachers must know how all the district initiatives are braided together under the framework of RTI. For example, every teacher should understand how collecting baseline data could be critical for design/analysis and decision making. A building RTI team must first spend time teaching the school as a whole the core concept of using multi-tiered problem solving to provide appropriate intervention to each child. Frankly, this is a rather foreign concept in most schools, which have used a factory approach and curricular adherence followed by a refer– test–place special education model. In those schools, teachers have been typically taught to adhere to core educational practices, rather than adjust educational practices based on outcome data. They have also been taught that children who fail should be serviced in some other place, or with some other label, rather than by altering practice in regular education. As such, it will likely take some time and effort to simply get a whole-school understanding and support implementation of an RTI model. If this time is not taken, it is unlikely the school will be successful.

Once a school has reached a full understating and support of the RTI theory, each group can be trained in specific applications necessary for their job. Some of this work has likely been accomplished. For example, many teachers have been trained in CBM, differentiated instruction, and EBIs. However, training is not enough. It is important that as school staff learn new skills, they receive "coaching" that provides feedback on the application of these skills. Many districts have various "coaches" in place to support the RTI framework. Some districts hire data coaches who assist various teams in collecting and interpreting data. Other districts hire coaches to (1) help teachers differentiate core instruction; (2) assist PSTs in designing, implementing, and evaluating interventions; and (3) provide expertise in reading and math instruction. Finally, schools that use a PBIS model should have a solid base of behavioral expertise. However, "behavioral" coaches are often hired to aid in implementation of the PBIS model.

Regardless of any preexisting knowledge, it is likely that much work will remain to prepare all school staff to implement RTI. For example, in our experience the concept of EBI is only loosely understood in schools. Specifically, there seem to be few teachers who use a function-based approach with children in need. To be fair, there have been essentially no practitioner-oriented intervention books that focus on selecting EBI based on function. In addition, most assessment training seems to have been limited to CBM, with a lack of focus on behavior and other academic areas. While training in CBM is necessary for RTI implementation, it is certainly not sufficient. In addition, there seems to be little focus on design and analysis once interventions have been attempted and outcome data collected. Finally, the critical step of decision making continues to elude many schools. For the RTI framework to be well implemented, building teams must utilize a problem-solving decision-making model. Each of these areas will likely require a great deal of attention. In the end, a well-trained team with some external support will have a good deal of work training a whole school. If this training process is considered a career-long professional development program for the whole school, it is a task that can be accomplished. On the upside, there will always be new aspects to learn and better ways to help children reach their full potential.

Yearly Retraining in Response-to-Intervention Best Practices

Once a school is up and running with an RTI model, the process of professional development should be altered to keep up to date with advancements. As outlined throughout the book, RTI is in a period of significant advancement and development. A number of states are currently implementing mandatory statewide RTI (e.g., Florida and Illinois). These large-scale rollouts will inevitability provide a significant amount of useful information about RTI. In addition, the National Canter for Response to Intervention and the new National Center for Intensive Interventions, along with other resources, have been producing and should continue to produce advancements in RTI technology. Finally, some school districts have been running RTI models for an extended amount of time. These districts are a cache of information about running an RTI model and should be sought out for their guidance. Indeed, this book was written with that thought in mind. When developing this book the first and second author understood it was essential to have a key player from a district with an extensive RTI history. The third author of this book was asked to contribute both for her ability to talk about what is done in an established RTI district, and also to discuss some of the ideas presented in this book. Indeed, one of the most enjoyable parts of writing this book was discussing how some of the more advanced topics in this book fit in established systems. These discussions resulted in some changes in how we suggest using methods such as SCD in the schools. We have found this process useful to advance our understanding of RTI, and believe such collaborations should be sought out in the future. In the end, considering the dynamic nature of the field, teams should consider and plan how they will keep current with RTI advancements and integrate what they learn into their school or district RTI model.

FINAL THOUGHTS

There is a great deal of excitement about the promise of RTI. In the last decade we have seen a tremendous development of the tools needed for RTI to be successful. We have also witnessed how many districts have harnessed the potential of RTI to create a more dynamic and effective approach to helping children learn. While it is easy to get excited about RTI, we would like to end this discussion of RTI professional development by emphasizing that complete implementation of the RTI framework usually takes 3 to 4 years and sometimes longer for secondary settings.

> While it is easy to get excited about RTI, it is a long-term process. Complete implementation of the RTI framework usually takes 3–4 years and sometimes longer for secondary settings.

It is important to remember that getting the system up and running will be a bumpy process, and it is likely that some colleagues will resist embracing this new approach. Throughout implementation it will be critical to evaluate the model and adjust using data to guide the way. In the end, system implementation of an RTI framework is very challenging work. Successful RTI systems are the result of a great deal of knowledge and leadership. Luckily, there are many talented educational professionals who are up to the challenge and embrace the opportunity to build a model that is truly responsive to the needs of children. It is within these talented teachers, administrators, school psychologists, and other educational professionals that the full potential of RTI will be realized and a whole generation of children will benefit.

Sample Response-to-Intervention Training Proposal

RATIONALE

With the reauthorization of IDEIA, states can no longer mandate that local educational agencies (LEAs) use an IQ–achievement discrepancy formula to qualify students for special education under the category of SLD. Instead, local districts may use an RTI approach as part of their evaluation process.

CURRENT NEEDS

LEAs planning to move toward an RTI approach as part of the SLD evaluation process will need to be trained on the core features of RTI in the context of a problem-solving model. LEAs will vary widely in their readiness to implement RTI. Each district will need training in the areas of measurement, problem solving, and curriculum adoption.

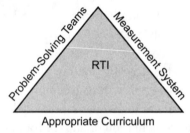

PROPOSAL

It is proposed to establish a problem-solving or RTI training center. The center would be hosted by a state-wide organization or a local district with expertise in the model. The center would help local districts and school sites transform their systems so that they deliver a research-based curriculum, use continuous and frequent measurement and organize their staff in cross-categorical teams with problem-solving expertise. The center would provide training using a "train the trainer" model but would incorporate a coaching approach so that the training results in meaningful system change. Schools seeking assistance would undergo assessment and be placed into one of three levels of development as described below. The center would be funded by state discretionary IDEIA funds and No Child Left Behind (NCLB) funds if available.

LEVELS OF TRAINING AND SUPPORT

Districts that wish to implement an RTI approach will need training and support organized around four strands:

- Strand 1: Orientation and introduction to RTI.
- Strand 2: Implementing a schoolwide measurement system.
- Strand 3: Research-based curriculum and instruction.
- Strand 4: Implementation of a problem-solving model.

Along with the four training strands, districts will be at one of four levels of implementation:

1. Level 1: District is exploring the use of RTI. Training is needed at all four strands.
2. Level 2: District wants pilot sites to assist with developing a formal RTI training plan. The district needs training on one or two of the core strands.
3. Level 3: District has a formal plan to adopt RTI but needs assistance on one or two of the strands. Technical assistance and training is needed around entitlement decisions.
4. Level 4: District has been using RTI to make special education entitlement decisions but needs coaching and training to ensure consistency across the district.

Each site team/district will complete a preassessment checklist to determine the level of training and support needed.

Level 1 Sites (Training Needed on All Four Strands)

Districts who are starting from scratch (i.e., need training in all four strands) will have a 4-year RTI adoption process as outlined below.

Year 1: Awareness Building and Establishing a Measurement System

- Targeted audience will attend a session to build awareness of RTI and related concepts. The target audience should include teams consisting of administrators, regular and special education teachers, and school psychologists.
- Targeted audience will attend a session to build awareness of the interface between RTI and NCLB. The target audience should include special education directors, principals, curriculum directors, and NCLB contacts.
- If teams determine they wish to become an RTI site, each building team will agree to establish and implement a schoolwide measurement system. Schools will attend five measurement training sessions and participate in a coaching component.
- Measurement sessions:
  - Session 1: Overview of general outcome measurement; problem identification; administration and scoring of measures.
  - Session 2: Preparing to do benchmark measurement: logistical issues.
  - Session 3: Interpreting benchmark measures; using the data to make decisions about strategic and intensive monitoring.
  - Session 4: Strategic and intensive monitoring: goal setting, graphing, survey-level assessment.
  - Session 5: Strategic and intensive monitoring: trend lines, decision-making rules, problem solution.

Year 2: Implementing a Core Literacy Curriculum

- Target audience will attend a session to build awareness of the big ideas in reading and how to select core curricula that address the big ideas (curriculum frameworks).
- District PST facilitators will attend five training sessions on the problem-solving model with a focus on academic issues. Team facilitators will receive this training one year earlier than the rest of their team. Team facilitators need to become fluent on the problem-solving process so they can provide leadership to their team. Team facilitators will act as "building-level coaches" during Year 3 when building teams are trained in the problem-solving model.
- Each building will continue implementing the measurement system with coaching. Each building will identify and/or establish a building-level PST to participate in Year 3 training (separate from existing special education teams).

Year 3: Problem-Solving Teams

- Target audience will attend five sessions on the problem-solving model and participate in a coaching component. School psychologists or other district coaches trained during Year 2 will deliver trainings and act as coaches.
- Each building will continue implementing the measurement system with coaching as needed.
- Coaches from the RTI center will observe during PST meetings and give feedback.
- Teams will begin using an RTI model for special education evaluations when the RTI center coach certifies that the team is ready (probably Year 4). In order to be "certified," teams will demonstrate that at least three cases have met all of the components necessary for problem solving.

Year 4: Response to Intervention with the Special Education Evaluation Component

- Each building will continue implementing the measurement system with coaching as needed.
- Each PST will meet regularly with a coaching component for LD eligibility decisions.
- PST facilitators will attend monthly network meetings with other facilitators and coaches.
- An RTI listserv will be established and maintained by the coaches.

Level 2 Sites (Training Needed on Some of the Response-to-Intervention Components)

- A needs assessment will be conducted to determine each district/building's area of need.
- Teams will attend trainings focused on their area of need (measurement, PST, or core curriculum strand).

Level 3 Sites (Sites Implementing All Three Response-to-Intervention Components)

- Each site team will complete a preassessment checklist and/or observation to determine the need for further problem-solving training.
- If PST meetings are established but the team has not been formally trained on the problem-solving model, the team will participate in five training sessions on the model and participate in coaching.
- If PSTs have been trained on the problem-solving model and are a certified RTI site, they will participate in coaching for one school year. Coaches will attend regular PST meetings, give feedback, and help with special education eligibility decisions.
- PST facilitators will attend monthly network meetings with other facilitators and coaches.

Level 4 Sites (Certified Response-to-Intervention Site)

- Each site team will complete a preassessment checklist to determine the need for additional training and support.

ESTIMATED RESOURCES NEEDED FOR IMPLEMENTATION OF TRAINING AND MANAGEMENT

Strand 1: Response-to-Intervention Orientation and Introduction

Model of Training

- Nine half-day sessions will be offered throughout the state by geographical region to build awareness of RTI and related concepts.

- Directors of special education and/or superintendents may request small-group sessions for principals and other administrative staff.
- Trainers may be able to do training for district staff (teaching staff), but this training will be at district expense and subject to trainer availability.

Strand 2: Establishing a Measurement System

Model of Training

- Districts identify a "measurement team" (e.g., building principal, school psychologist, special education teacher, regular education teacher) to attend a 5-day measurement institute offered during the summer and/or school year.
- Districts will be assigned "measurement coaches" to assist in implementation. Coaches will provide assistance on site and through regular contact with the "lead measurement contact" for each building.
- Districts will have access to a measurement listserv.
- Districts will receive "start-up" revenue to purchase a data management system.

Strand 3: Curriculum and Instruction

Model of Training

- Districts will identify a "lead district coach" and coaches for each building in the district.
- Coaches will attend a 5-day training session organized around the five dimensions of reading instruction and understand how they interrelate.
- Coaches will attend a 1-day session on evaluating core, supplemental, and intervention curricula in grades K–3.
- Each workshop will have a "module" that includes a PowerPoint presentation, activities, and materials.
- The district coach and building-level coaches will train district staff using the modules.
- District coaches will observe reading instruction provided by classroom teachers and provide feedback.
- During Year 2, the district and building coaches will attend a monthly networking and problem-solving meeting.
- During Year 2, a coach from the RTI center will visit each building site three times and provide feedback to coaches on their classroom coaching skills.

Strand 4: Problem-Solving Model

Model of Training

- Districts identify a "lead district coach" and coaches for each building in the district.
- The lead district coach and building-level coaches attend a five-session "train the trainer" workshop on the problem-solving model.
- Each workshop will have a "module" that includes a PowerPoint presentation, activities, and materials.
- The district coach and building-level coaches will train district staff the following year (Year 2) using the modules.
- During Year 2, a coach from the RTI center will visit each building's PST three times and provide feedback to teams on the problem-solving process.
- During Year 2, districts will identify a .5 FTE RTI coordinator.
- During Year 2, the district RTI coordinator and coaches will attend a monthly networking and problem-solving meeting.
- Coaches will have access to a problem-solving listserv.

SAMPLE RTI SCHEDULE

Strand	Target audience	Session name	Outcomes of session	Sessions offered	Coaching component
Awareness	District leadership team, building leadership team, all staff	Response to Intervention: The Interrelationship between NCLB and IDEIA	1. Participants will understand the interface between RTI and NCLB. 2. Participants will understand the necessary components of RTI and problem solving. 3. Participants will understand the necessity of providing an adequate core curriculum as the basis for prevention of academic problems. 4. Participants will understand the necessity of having a measurement system in place for screening and progress monitoring. 5. Participants will understand the necessity of having effective problem-solving systems in place.	9	No
Measurement	Building leadership team, grade-level teams	Session 1/5—Overview of General Outcome Measurement	1. Participants will understand the conceptual foundations of general outcome measurement (GOM). 2. Participants will be proficient in administering and scoring GOM in the areas of reading, math, written expression, and early literacy. 3. Participants will understand the application of GOM in relation to behavior. 4. Participants will understand how GOMs fit within the problem identification stage of the problem-solving model. 5. Applied assignment for next session TBD.	1	Yes
Measurement	Building leadership team, grade-level teams	Session 2/5—Preparing to do Benchmark Measurement: Logistical Issues	1. Participants will identify the logistical steps necessary to collect benchmark data. 2. Participants will leave this session with a detailed plan for collecting benchmark data in their building. 3. Applied assignment for next session TBD.	1	Yes
Measurement	Building leadership team, grade-level teams, problem-solving teams	Session 3/5—Interpreting Benchmark Measures: Using Data to Make Decisions	1. Participants will understand how to use benchmark data to identify students in need of strategic and intensive monitoring. 2. Participants will understand how to conduct a survey-level assessment. 3. Applied assignment for next session TBD.	1	Yes

150

Measurement	Problem-solving teams	Session 4/5—Strategic and Intensive Monitoring Issues	1. Participants will understand the difference between long-term and short-term measurement. 2. Participants will understand how to use GOMs to write measurable goals. 3. Participants will understand how to graph GOM data. 4. Applied assignment for next session TBD.	1	Yes
Measurement	Problem-solving teams	Session 5/5—Problem-Solution Decisions	1. Participants will understand how to use GOM data to determine program effectiveness. 2. Participants will understand data-based decision-making rules. 3. Participants will understand how to use GOM data to determine whether a problem has been solved. 4. Applied assignment for next session TBD.	1	Yes
Problem-solving teams	Problem-solving teams, instructional coaches	Session 1/5—Problem-Solving Team Training: Overview and Problem Identification	1. Teams will identify the steps of the problem-solving model. 2. Teams will identify the question be answered in the problem identification stage and assessment activities conducted at this stage. 3. Teams will identify the assessment activities associated with RIOT (review, interview, observe, test). 4. Teams will demonstrate their ability to write discrepancy statements. 5. Applied assignment: Teams will select at least one student from their school and collect problem identification data prior to Session 2.	1	Yes
Problem-solving teams	Problem-solving teams, instructional coaches	Session 2/5—Problem-Solving Team Training: Problem Analysis	1. Teams will understand the advanced theory of problem analysis and specific techniques for curriculum-based evaluation in order to determine *why* identified problems are occurring. 2. Teams will identify the five common reasons students experience academic failure. 3. Teams will identify the common reasons students experience behavior problems. 4. Teams will understand the need to assess the instruction, curriculum, environment, and learner (ICEL) in determining why problems are occurring. 5. Applied assignment: Teams will collect any additional data needed to develop a data-based hypothesis for why their selected student's problem is occurring prior to session.	1	Yes

Strand	Target audience	Session name	Outcomes of session	Sessions offered	Coaching component
Problem-solving teams	Problem-solving teams, instructional coaches	Session 3/5—Problem-Solving Team Training: Plan Development	1. Participants will understand how to write goal statements for individual students. 2. Participants will understand how to write specific intervention plans for students. 3. Participants will understand how to select or create a progress monitoring plan. 4. Applied assignment: Teams will design and begin implementation of a plan for their selected student prior to Session 4.	1	Yes
Problem-solving teams	Problem-solving teams, instructional coaches	Session 4/5—Problem-Solving Team Training: Plan Implementation	1. Teams will understand how to select research-based interventions that are well matched to student problems. 2. Teams will understand techniques for ensuring implementation integrity. 3. Applied assignment: Teams will continue to collect data on their selected student, and have at least eight data points prior to Session 5.	1	Yes
Problem-solving teams	Problem-solving teams, instructional coaches	Session 5/5—Problem-Solving Team Training: Plan Evaluation	1. Teams will understand how to apply decision-making rules in order to evaluate plan effectiveness. 2. Teams will learn a framework for systematically evaluating data and altering intervention plans as needed to increase student achievement.	1	Yes
Facilitator meetings	Facilitators of problem-solving teams		1. Facilitators of problem-solving teams will network with other facilitators and coaches on a monthly basis to discuss implementation issues.	Monthly	Yes
Core curriculum and literacy	District literacy team	Implementing an Effective Beginning Reading Curriculum	1. Participants will attend five sessions. 2. Each session will focus on one of the five dimensions of reading instruction and understand how they interrelate. 3. Participants will understand research-based principles for effective instruction in each of the five dimensions. 4. Participants will understand a framework for organizing school resources to maximize effectiveness of instruction for all students. 5	Yes	
Core curriculum and literacy	District literacy team	A Consumer's Guide for Evaluating Core, Supplemental, and Intervention Curricula	1. Teams will become proficient with a standardized framework for evaluating curriculum.	1	Yes

References

Aaron, P. G. (1997). The impending demise of the discrepancy formula. *Review of Educational Research 67*, 461–502.

Afflerbach, P. (2007). Teacher Questioning as Assessment. In *Understanding and using reading assessment, K–12* (pp. 51–71). Newark, DE: International Reading Association.

Alberto, P., & Troutman, A. C. (2006). *Applied behavior analysis for teachers* (7th ed.). Upper Saddle River, NJ: Merrill Prentice Hall.

American Educational Research Association, American Psychological Association, and National Council for Measurement in Education. (1999). *Standards for educational and psychological testing.* Washington, DC: American Educational Research Association.

Ardoin, S. P., & Christ, T. J. (2009). Curriculum-based measurement of oral reading: Estimates of standard error when monitoring progress using alternate passage sets. *School Psychology Review, 38,* 266–283.

Audi, R. (Ed.). (1999). *The Cambridge dictionary of philosophy* (2nd ed.). New York: Cambridge University Press.

August, D., Carlo, M., Dressler, C., & Snow, C. (2005). The critical role of vocabulary development for English language learners. *Learning Disabilities Research and Practice 20,* 50–57.

Baer, D. M., Wolf, M. M., & Risley, T. R. (1968). Some current dimensions of applied behavior analysis. *Journal of Applied Behavior Analysis, 1,* 91–97

Barrish, H. H., Saunders, M., & Wolf, M. M. (1969). Good behavior game: effects of individual contingencies for group consequences on disruptive behavior in a classroom. *Journal of Applied Behavior Analysis, 2,* 119–124.

Batsche, G., Elliott, J., Graden, J. L., Grimes, J., Kovaleski, J. F., Prasse, D., et al. (2006). *Response to intervention: Policy considerations and implementation.* Alexandria, VA: National Association of State Directors of Special Education.

Batsche, G., Kavale, K. A., & Kovaleski, J. F. (2006). Competing views: A dialogue on response to intervention. *Assessment for Effective Intervention, 32,* 6–19.

Berninger, V. W., Abbott, R. D., Vermeulen, K., & Fulton, C. M. (2006). Paths to reading comprehension in at-risk second-grade readers. *Journal of Learning Disabilities, 39,* 334–351.

Betts, E. A. (1946). *Foundations of reading instruction.* New York: American Book.

Bloom, B. S., Hastings, J. T., & Madaus, G. F. (1971). *Handbook on formative and summative evaluation of student learning.* New York: McGraw-Hill.

Bonfiglio, C. M., Daly, E. J., Martens, B. K. Lin, L. R., & Corsaut, S. (2004). An experimental analysis of reading interventions: Generalization across instructional strategies, time, and passages. *Journal of Applied Behavior Analysis, 37,* 111–114.

Bradley, R., Danielson, L., & Hallahan, D. P. (Eds.). (2002). *Identification of learning disabilities: Research to practice.* Mahwah, NJ: Erlbaum.

Bradley-Johnson, S., & Lesiak, J. L. (1989). *Problems in written expression: Assessment and Remediation.* New York: Guilford Press.

Bransford, J. D. & Stein, B. S. (1984). *The IDEAL problem solver.* New York: Freeman.

Brown-Chidsey, R. (2007). No more "waiting to fail." *Educational Leadership, 65*(2), 40–46.

Brown-Chidsey, R. & Steege, M. W. (2010). *Response to intervention: Principles and strategies for effective practice* (2nd ed.). New York: Guilford Press.

Burns, M. K. (2004). Empirical analysis of drill ratio research: Refining the instructional level for drill tasks. *Remedial and Special Education, 25,* 167–175.

Burns, M. K. (2007). Reading at the instructional level with children identified as learning disabled: Potential implications for response-to-intervention. *School Psychology Quarterly, 22,* 297–313.

Burns, M. K., Appleton, J. J., & Stehouwer, J. D. (2005). Meta-analysis of response-to-intervention research: Examining field-based and research-implemented models. *Journal of Psychoeducational Assessment, 23,* 381–394.

Burns, M. K., Codding, R. S., Boice, C. H., & Lukito, G. (2010). Meta-analysis of acquisition and fluency math interventions with instructional and frustration level skills: Evidence for a skill by treatment interaction. *School Psychology Review, 39,* 69–83.

Burns, M. K., Deno, S. L., & Jimerson, S. R. (2007). Toward a unified response-to-intervention model. In S. R. Jimerson, M. K. Burns, & A. VanDerHeyden (Eds.), *Handbook of response to intervention* (pp. 428–440). New York: Springer.

Burns, M. K., & Gibbons, K. (2012). *Implementing response-to-intervention in elementary and secondary schools: Procedures to assure scientific-based practices* (2nd ed.). New York: Routledge.

Burns, M. K., Jacob, S., & Wagner, A. (2008). Ethical and legal issues associate with using response-to-intervention to assess learning disabilities. *Journal of School Psychology, 46,* 263–279.

Burns, M. K., Kanive, R., & Degrande, M. (2012). Effect of a computer-delivered math fact intervention as a supplemental intervention for math in third and fourth grades. *Remedial and Special Education, 33,* 184–191.

Burns, M. K., Peters, R., & Noell, G. H. (2008). Using performance feedback to enhance the implementation integrity of the problem-solving team process. *Journal of School Psychology, 46,* 537–550.

Burns, M. K., & Scholin, S. (2012). Relationship between pre-intervention data and post-intervention reading fluency and growth: A meta-analysis of assessment data for individual students. *Psychology in the Schools, 49,* 385–398.

Burns, M. K., Scholin, S. E., Kosciolek, S., & Livingston, J. (2010). Reliability of decision-making frameworks for response to intervention for reading. *Journal of Psychoeducational Assessment, 28,* 102–114.

Burns, M. K., & Senesac, B. K. (2005). Comparison of dual discrepancy criteria for diagnosis of unresponsiveness to intervention. *Journal of School Psychology, 43,* 393–406.

Burns, M. K., Tucker, J. A., Frame, J., Foley, S., & Hauser, A. (2000). Interscorer, alternate-form, internal consistency, and test–retest reliability of Gickling's model of curriculum-based assessment for reading. *Journal of Psychoeducational Assessment, 18,* 353–360.

Burns, M. K., & VanDerHeyden, A. M. (2006). Using response to intervention to assess learning disabilities: Introduction to the special series. *Assessment for Effective Intervention, 32,* 3–5.

Burns, M. K., VanDerHeyden, A. M., & Boice, C. H. (2008). Best practices in delivering intensive academic interventions for individual students. In A. Thomas & J. Grimes (Eds.), *Best practices in school psychology V* (pp. 1151–1162.). Bethesda, MD: National Association of School Psychologists.

Burns, M. K., VanDerHeyden, A. M., & Jiban, C (2006). Assessing the instructional level for mathematics: A comparison of methods. *School Psychology Review, 35,* 401–418.

Burns, M. K. & Wagner, D. (2008). Determining an effective intervention within a brief experimental analysis for reading: A meta-analytic review. *School Psychology Review, 37,* 126–136.

Burns, M. K., Wiley, H. I., Viglietta, E. (2008). Best practices in facilitating problem-solving teams. In A. Thomas & J. Grimes (Eds.), *Best practices in school psychology V* (Vol. 5, pp. 1633–1644). Bethesda, MD: National Association of School Psychologists.

Busk, P. L., & Serlin, R. C. (1992). Meta-analysis for single-case research. In T. R. Kratochwill & J. R. Levin (Eds.), *Single-case research design and analysis: New directions for psychology and education* (pp. 187–212). Hillsdale, NJ: Erlbaum.

Carnine, D. (2003, March). IDEA: Focusing on improving results for children with disabilities. Testimony in Hearing before the Subcommittee on Education Reform, Committee on Education and the Workforce, United States House of Representatives.

Carson, P. M., & Eckert, T. L. (2003). An experimental analysis of mathematics instructional components: Examining the effects of student-selected versus empirically selected interventions. *Journal of Behavioral Education, 12*(1), 35–54.

Carter, S. L., Devlin, S., Doggett, R. A., Harber, M. M., & Barr, C. (2004). Determining the influence of tangible items on screaming and handmouthing following an inconclusive functional analysis. *Behavioral Interventions, 19,* 51–58.

Chafouleas, S. M., Riley-Tillman, T. C., & Christ, T. J. (2009). Direct behavior rating (DBR): An merging method for assessing social behavior within a tiered intervention system. *Assessment for Effective Intervention, 34,* 195–200.

Chafouleas, S. M., Riley-Tillman, T. C., & Eckert, T. (2003). A comparison of school psychologists' acceptability of norm-referenced, curriculum-based, and brief experimental analysis methods to assess reading. *School Psychology Review, 32,* 272–281.

Chafouleas, S. M, Riley-Tillman, T. C., & Sugai, G. (2007). *School-based behavioral assessment: Informing intervention and instruction.* New York: Guilford Press.

Chafouleas, S. M., Sanetti, L. M. H., Kilgus, S. P., & Maggin, D. M. (2112). Evaluating sensitivity to behavioral change across consultation cases using Direct Behavior Rating Single-Item Scales (DBR-SIS). *Exceptional Children, 78,* 491–505.

Christ, T. J. (2006). Short-term estimates of growth using curriculum-based measurement of oral reading fluency: Estimating standard error of the slope to construct confidence intervals. *School Psychology Review, 35,* 128–133.

Christ, T. J. (2008). Best practices in problem analysis. In A. Thomas & J. Grimes (Eds.), *Best practices in school psychology V* (Vol. 2, pp. 154–176). Bethesda, MD: National Association of School Psychologists.

Christ, T. J., Johnson-Gros, K., & Hintze, J. M. (2005). An examination of computational fluency: The reliability of curriculum-based outcomes within the context of educational decisions. *Psychology in the Schools, 42,* 615–622.

Codding, R. S., Burns, M. K., & Lukito, G. (2011). Meta-analysis of mathematic computation fluency interventions: A component analysis. *Learning Disability Research and Practice, 26,* 36–47.

Cohen, J. (1988). *Statistical power analysis for the behavioral sciences* (2nd ed.). Hillsdale, NJ: Erlbaum.

Cooper, J. O., Heron, T. E., & Heward, W. L. (2007). *Applied behavior analysis.* Upper Saddle River, NJ: Pearson Education.

Daly, E. J. III, Martens, B. K., Hamler, K., R., Dool, E. J., & Eckert, T. L. (1999). A brief experimental analysis for identifying instructional components needed to improve oral reading fluency. *Journal of Applied Behavior Analysis, 32,* 83-94.

Daly, E. J. III, Martens, B. K., Kilmer, A., & Massie, D. (1996). The effects of instructional match and content overlap on generalized reading performance. *Journal of Applied Behavioral Analysis, 29,* 507–518.

Daly, E. J. III, Witt, J. C., Martens, B. K., & Dool, E. J. (1997). A model for conducting a functional analysis of academic performance problems. *School Psychology Review, 26,* 554–574.

Deno, S. L. (1985). Curriculum-based measurement: The emerging alternative. *Exceptional Children, 52,* 219–232.

Deno, S. (2002). School psychologist as problem solver. In A. Thomas & J. Grimes (Eds.), *Best practices in school psychology IV* (pp. 37–56). Washington, DC: National Association of School Psychologists.

Deno, S. L. (2003). Developments in curriculum-based measurement. *Journal of Special Education, 37,* 184–192.

Deno, S. L. (2013). Problem-solving assessment. In R. Brown-Chidsey & K. Andren (Eds.), *Assessment for intervention: A problem-solving approach* (2nd ed., pp. 10–36). New York: Guilford Press.

Deno, S. L., & Mirkin, P. K. (1977). *Data-based program modification: A manual.* Reston, VA: Council for Exceptional Children.

Donovan, M. S., & Cross, C. T. (2002). *Minority students in special and gifted education.* Washington, DC: National Academics Press.

Duhon, G. J., Noell, G. H., Witt, J. C., Freeland, J. T., Dufrene, B. A., & Gilbertson, D. N. (2004). Identifying academic skills and performance deficits: The experimental analysis of brief assessments of academic skills. *School Psychology Review, 33,* 429–443.

DuPaul, G. J., & Stoner, G. (2003). *ADHD in the schools: Assessment and intervention strategies* (3rd ed.). New York: Guilford Press.

Eckert, T. L., Ardoin, S. P., Daisey, D. M., & Scarola, M. D. (2000). Empirically evaluating the effectiveness of reading interventions: The use of brief experimental analysis and single case designs. *Psychology in the Schools, 37,* 463–473.

Eckert, T. L., Ardoin, S. P., Daly, E. J. III, & Martens, B. K. (2002). Improving oral reading fluency: A brief experimental analysis of combining an antecedent intervention with consequences. *Journal of Applied Behavior Analysis, 35,* 271–281.

Fabiano, G. A., Pelham, W. E., Coles, E. K., Gnagy, E. M., Chronis-Tuscano, A., & O'Connor, B. C. (2009). A meta-analysis of behavoral treatments for attention-deficit/hyperactivity disorder. *Clinical Psychology Review, 29,* 129–140.

Feifer, S. G. (2008). Integrating response to intervention (RTI) with neuropsychology: A scientific approach to reading. *Psychology in the Schools, 45,* 812–825.

Fiorello, C. A., Hale, J. B., & Snyder, L. E. (2006). Cognitive hypothesis testing and response to intervention for children with reading problems. *Psychology in the Schools, 43,* 835–853.

Finn, C. E., Jr., Rotherham, R. A. J., & Hokansen, C. R., Jr. (Eds.). (2001). *Rethinking special education for a new century.* Washington, DC: Thomas B. Fordham Foundation and Progressive Policy Institute.

Fletcher, J. M., Francis, D. J., Shaywitz, S. E., Lyon, G. R., Foorman, B. R., Stuebing, K. K., et al. (1998). Intelligence testing and the discrepancy model for children with learning disabilities. *Learning Disabilities Research and Practice, 13,* 186–203.

Fuchs, L. S., & Fuchs, D. (1986). Effects of systematic formative evaluation: A meta-analysis. *Exceptional Children, 53,* 199–208.

Fuchs, L., & Deno, S. (1991). Paradigmatic distinctions between instructionally relevant measurement models. *Exceptional Children, 57,* 488–500.

Fuchs, D., & Fuchs, L. S. (1998). Researchers and teachers working together to adapt instruction for diverse learners. *Learning Disabilities Research and Practice, 13,* 126–137.

Fuchs, L. S., Fuchs, D., Prentice, K., Burch, M., Hamlett, C. L., Owen, R., et al. (2003). Explicitly teaching for transfer: Effects on third-grade students' mathematical problem solving. *Journal of Educational Psychology, 95,* 293–305.

Gansle, K. A., & McMahon, C. M. (1997). Component integrity of teacher intervention management behavior using a student self-monitoring treatment: An experimental analysis. *Journal of Behavioral Education, 7,* 405–419.

Gansle, K. A., & Noell, G. H. (2007). The fundamental role of intervention implementation in assessing response to intervention. In S. R. Jimerson, M. K. Burns, & A. M. VanDerHeyden (Eds.), *Response to intervention: The science and practice of assessment and intervention* (pp. 244–251). New York: Springer.

Gibbons, K., & Howe, K. (2000, January). *The effects of monitoring student progress on grade-level material versus goal-level material.* Paper presented at the symposium Using Curriculum-Based Measurement at the National, State, and District Levels for Accountability Decisions, Pacific Coast Research Conference, La Jolla, CA.

Gickling, E. E., & Armstrong, D. L. (1978). Levels of instructional difficulty as related to on-task behavior, task completion, and comprehension. *Journal of Learning Disabilities, 11,* 559–566.

Gickling, E. E., & Havertape, S. (1981). *Curriculum-based assessment (CBA).* Minneapolis, MN: School Psychology Inservice Training Network.

Gickling, E., & Thompson, V. (1985). A personal view of curriculum-based assessment. *Exceptional Children, 52,* 205–218.

Gravois, T. A., & Gickling, E. E. (2008). Best practices in instructional assessment. In A. Thomas & J. Grimes (Eds.), *Best practices in school psychology V* (Vol. 2, pp. 503–518). Bethesda, MD: National Association of School Psychologists.

Gresham, F. M. (2002). Responsiveness to intervention: An alternative approach to the identification of learning disabilities. In R. Bradley & L. Danielson (Eds.), *Identification of learning disabilities: Research to practice* (pp. 467–519). Mahwah, NJ: Erlbaum.

Hale, J. B., Fiorello, C. A., Bertin, M., & Sherman, R. (2003). Predicting math achievement through neuropsychological interpretation of the WISC-III variance components. *Journal of Psychoeducational Assessment, 21,* 358–380.

Hale, J. B., Fiorello, C. A., Kavanagh, J. A., Hoeppner, J. B., & Gaither, R. A. (2001). WISC-III predictors of academic achievement for children with learning disabilities: Are global and factor scores comparable? *School Psychology Quarterly, 16,* 31–55.

Hammill, D. D., Wiederholt, J. L., & Allen, E. A. (2007). *Test of silent contextual reading fluency.* Austin, TX: Pro-Ed.

Haring, N. G., & Eaton, M. D. (1978). Systematic instructional technology: An instructional hierarchy. In N. G. Haring, T. C. Lovitt, M. D. Eaton, & C. L. Hansen (Eds.), *The fourth R: Research in the classroom* (pp. 23–40). Columbus, OH: Merrill.

Heartland Area Education Agency 11. (2004). *Heartland AEA 11 annual progress report.* Johnston, IA: Author.

Horner, R. H. (2008). *IES single-case design training institute.* Washington, DC.

Horner, R. H., Carr, E. G., Halle, J., McGee, G., Odom, S, & Wolery, M. (2005). The use of single-subject research to identify evidence-based practice in special education. *Exceptional Children, 71*(2), 165–179.

Hosp, J. L. (2008). Best practices in aligning academic assessment with instruction. In A. Thomas & J. Grimes (Eds.), *Best practices in school psychology V* (Vol. 2, pp. 363–376). Bethesda, MD: National Association of School Psychologists.

Hosp, J. L., & Ardoin, S. P. (2008). Assessment for instructional planning. *Assessment for Effective Intervention, 33,* 69–77

Hosp, M. K., Hosp, J. L., & Howell, K. W. (2007). *The ABCs of CBM: A practical guide to curriculum-based measurement.* New York: Guilford Press.

Hosp, M. K., & MacConnell, K. L. (2008). Best practiecs in curriculum-based evaluation in early reading. In A. Thomas & J. Grimes (Eds.), *Best practices in school psychology V* (Vol. 2, pp. 377–396). Bethesda, MD: National Association of School Psychologists.

Howell, K. W. (2008). Best practices in curriculum-based evaluation and advanced reading. In A. Thomas & J. Grimes (Eds.), *Best practices in school psychology V* (Vol. 2, pp. 397–418). Bethesda, MD: National Association of School Psychologists.

Howell, K. W., Hosp, J. L., & Kurns, S. (2008). Best practices in curriculum-based evaluation. In A. Thomas & J. Grimes (Eds.) *Best practices in school psychology V* (Vol. 2, pp. 349–362). Bethesda, MD: National Association of School Psychologists.

Howell, K. W., & Nolet, V. (2000). Tools for assessment. In *Curriculum-based evaluation: Teaching and decision making* (3rd ed.). Scarborough, ON, Canada: Wadsworth/Thompson Learning.

Ikeda, M. J., Neessen, E., & Witt, J. C. (2008). Best practices in universal screening. In A. Thomas & J. Grimes (Eds.), *Best practices in school psychology V* (Vol. 2, pp. 103–114). Bethesda, MD: National Association of School Psychologists.

Ikeda, M. J., Rahn-Blakeslee, R., Neibling, B. C., Gustafson, J. K., Allison, R., & Stumme, J. (2007). The Heartland Area Education Agency 11 problem-solving approach: An overview and lessons learned. In S. R. Jimerson, M. K. Burns, & A. M. VanDerHeyden (Eds.), *Handbook of response to intervention: The science and practice of assessment and intervention* (pp. 255–268). New York: Springer.

Iwata B. A., Dorsey M. F., Slifer K. J., Bauman K. E., & Richman G. S. (1982). Toward a functional analysis of self-injury. *Analysis and Intervention in Developmental Disabilities, 2,* 3–20.

Jenkins, J. (2003, December). *Candidate measures for screening at-risk students.* Paper presented at the National Research Center on Learning Disabilities Responsiveness-to-Intervention Symposium, Kansas City, MO.

Jenkins, J. R., Hudson, R. F., & Johnson, E. S. (2007). Screening for at-risk readers in a response to intervention framework. *School Psychology Review, 36*(4), 582–600.

Jimerson, S., Burns, M. K., & VanDerHeyden, A. M. (Eds.). (2007). *The handbook of response to intervention: The science and practice of assessment and intervention.* New York: Springer.

Johnston, J. M., & Pennypacker, H. S. (1980). *Strategies and tactics of human behavioral research.* Hillsdale, NJ: Erlbaum.

Jones, K. M., & Wickstrom, K. F. (2002). Done in sixty seconds: Further analysis of the brief assessment model for academic problems. *School Psychology Review, 31,* 554–568.

Kaufman, C. J., & Flicek, M. (1995, March). *Treatment integrity in school-based behavioral consultation and its relationship with treatment efficacy and acceptability.* Paper presented at the 27th annual convention of the National Association of School Psychologists, Chicago.

Kavale, K. A., & Forness, S. R. (1999). Effectiveness of special education. In C. R. Reynolds & T. B. Gutkin (Eds.), *The handbook of school psychology* (3rd ed., pp. 984–1024). New York: Wiley.

Kazdin, A.E. (2011). *Single-case research designs: Methods for clinical and applied settings* (2nd ed.). New York: Oxford University Press.

Kelley, B. (2008). Best practices in curriculum-based evaluation and math. In A. Thomas & J. Grimes (Eds.), *Best practices in school psychology V* (Vol. 2, pp. 417–438). Bethesda, MD: National Association of School Psychologists.

Ketterlin-Geller, L. R., & Yovanoff, P. (2009). Diagnostic assessments in mathematics to support instructional decision making. *Practical Assessment, Research and Evaluation, 14,* 1–11.

Kilpatrick, J., Swafford, J., & Finell, B. (Eds.). (2001). *Adding it up: Helping children learn mathematics.* Washington, DC: National Academies Press.

Kovaleski, J. F, Gickling, E. E., & Morrow, H. (1998). High versus low implementation of instructional support teams: A case for maintaining program fidelity. *Remedial and Special Education, 20,* 170–183.

Linn, R. L., & Grolund, N. E. (2000). *Measurement and assessment in teaching* (8th ed.). Upper Saddle River, NJ: Merrill/Prentice Hall.

Lyon, G. R., Fletcher, J. M., Shaywitz, S. E., Shaywitz, B. A., Torgesen, J. K., & Wood, F. B. (2001). Rethinking learning disabilities. In C. E. Finn, Jr., A. J. Rotherham, & C. R. Hokanson, Jr. (Eds.), *Rethinking special education for a new century* (pp. 259–287). Washington, DC: Thomas B. Fordham Foundation.

Mace, F. C., Yankanich, M. A., & West, B. J. (1988). Toward a methodology of experimental analysis and treatment of aberrant classroom behaviors. *Special Services in the Schools, 4,* 71–88.

Maggin, D. M., Chafouleas, S. M., Mosely, K. M., & Johnson, A. J. (2011). A systematic evaluation of token economies as a classroom management tool for students with challenging behavior. *Journal of School Psychology, 49,* 529–554.

Maggin, D. M., Johnson, A. H., Chafouleas, S. M., Ruberto, L. M., & Berggren, M. (in press). A systematic evidence review of school-based group contingency interventions for students with challenging behavior. *Journal of School Psychology.*

Marston, D. B. (1989). A curriculum-based measurement approach to assessing academic performance: What it is and why do it. In M. R. Shinn (Ed.), *Curriculum-based measurement: Assessing special children* (pp. 18–78). New York: Guilford Press.

Marston, D. (2003, December). *Comments on three papers addressing the question: "How many tiers are needed within RTI to achieve acceptable prevention outcomes and to achieve acceptable patterns of LD identification?"* Paper presented at the National Research Center on Learning Disabilities Responsiveness-to-Intervention Symposium, Kansas City, MO.

Marston, D., Muyskens, P., Lau, M., & Canter, A. (2003). Problem-solving model for decision making with high-incidence disabilities: The Minneapolis experience. *Learning Disabilities Research and Practice, 18,* 187–200.

Marzano, R. (2003). Two wrongs and a right. *Educational Leadership, 60*(5), 56–60.

McComas, J. J., Hoch, H., & Mace, F. C. (2000). Functional analysis. In E. S. Shapiro & T. R. Kratochwill (Eds.), *Conducting school-based assessments of child and adolescent behavior* (pp. 78–120). New York: Guilford Press.

McComas, J. J., & Mace, F. C. (2000). Theory and practice in conducting functional analysis. In E. S. Shapiro & T. R. Kratochwill (Eds.), *Behavioral assessment in schools: Theory, research, and clinical foundations* (2nd ed., pp. 78–103). New York: Guilford Press.

McComas, J. J., Wacker, D. P., Cooper, L. J., Asmus, J. M., Richman, D., & Stoner, B. (1996). Brief experimental analysis of stimulus prompts for accurate responding on academic tasks in an outpatient clinic. *Journal of Applied Behavior Analysis, 29,* 397–401.

McNamara, K., & Hollinger, C. (2003). Intervention-based assessment: Evaluation rates and eligibility findings. *Exceptional Children, 69,* 181–194.

Messick, S. (1995). Validity of psychological assessment: Validation of inferences from persons' responses and performances as scientific inquiry into score meaning. *American Psychologist, 50,* 741–749.

Moncher, F. J., & Prinz, F. J. (1991). Treatment fidelity in outcome studies. *Clinical Psychology Review, 11,* 247–266.

National Mathematics Advisory Panel. (2008). *Foundations for success: The final report of the National Mathematics Advisory Panel.* Washington, DC: U.S. Department of Education.

National Reading Panel. (2000). *Report of the National Reading Panel. Teaching children to read: An evidence-based assessment of the scientific research literature on reading and its implications for reading instruction* (NIH Publication No. 00-4769). Washington, DC: U.S. Government Printing Office.

Noell, G. H. (2008). Research examining the relationships among consultation process, treatment integrity, and outcomes. In W. P. Erchul & S. M. Sheridan (Eds.), *Handbook of research in school consultation: Empirical foundations for the field* (pp. 315–334). Mahwah, NJ: Erlbaum.

Noell, G. H., Duhon, G. J., Gatti, S. L., & Connell, J. E. (2002). Consultation, follow-up, and implementation of behavior management interventions in general education. *School Psychology Review, 31,* 217–234.

Noell, G. H. Freeland, J. T., Witt, J. C., & Gansle, K. A. (2001). Using brief assessments to identify effective interventions for individual students. *Journal of School Psychology, 39,* 335–355.

Noell, G. H., & Gansle, K. A. (2006). Assuring the form has substance: Treatment plan implementation as the foundation of assessing response to intervention. *Assessment for Effective Intervention, 32,* 32–39.

Northwest Evaluation Association. (2003). *Technical manual for the NWEA measures of academic progress and achievement level tests.* Lake Oswego, OR: Author.

Parker, D. C., Burns, M. K., & McComas, J. J. (2012). *Comparison of instructional level metrics with students identified as at-risk for reading failure.* Manuscript submitted for publication.

Parker, R. I., & Hagan-Burke, S. (2007). Useful effect size interpretations for single-case research. *Behavior Therapy, 38,* 95–105.

Parker, R. I., Hagan-Burke, S., & Vannest, K. (2007). Percentage of all non-overlapping data (PAND): An alternative to PND. *Journal of Special Education 40,* 194–204.

Parker, R. I., Vannest, K. J., & Brown, L. (2009). The improvement rate difference for single-case research. *Exceptional Children, 75,* 135–150.

Pearson. (2010). *AIMSweb.* Bloomington, MN: Author.

President's Commission on Excellence in Special Education. (2001). *A new era: Revitalizing special education for children and their families.* Washington, DC: U.S. Department of Education.

Renaissance Learning. (2011). *STAR early literacy.* Wisconsin Rapids: Author.

Reschly, D. J. (1996). Functional assessments and special education decision making. In W. Stainback & S. Stainback (Eds.), *Controversial issues confronting special education: Divergent perspectives* (2nd ed., pp. 115–128). Boston: Allyn & Bacon.

Reschly, D. J., & Ysseldyke, J. E. (2002). Paradigm shift: The past is not the future. In A. Thomas & J. Grimes (Eds.), *Best practices in school psychology IV* (pp. 3–21). Bethesda, MD: National Association of School Psychologists.

Riley-Tillman, T. C., & Burns, M. K. (2009). *Evaluating educational interventions: Single-case design for measuring response to intervention.* New York: Guilford Press.

Riley-Tillman, T. C., Chafouleas, S. M., Christ, T., Briesch, A. M., & LeBel, T. J. (2009). Impact of wording and behavioral specificity on the accuracy of direct behavior rating scales (DBRs). *School Psychology Quarterly, 24,* 1–12.

Riley-Tillman, T. C., Chafouleas, S. M., Sassu, K. A., Chanese, J. A. M., & Glazer, A. D. (2008). Examining the agreement of direct behavior ratings and systematic direct observation for on-task and disruptive behavior. *Journal of Positive Behavior Interventions, 10,* 136–143.

Riley-Tillman, T. C., Methe, S. A., & Weegar, K. (2009). Examining the use of direct behavior rating methodology on classwide formative assessment: A case study. *Assessment for Effective Intervention, 34*, 224–230.

Riley-Tillman, T. C., & Walcott, C. M. (2007). Using baseline logic to maximize the value of educational interventions. *School Psychology Forum, 1*(2), 87–97.

Runes, D. D. (Ed.). (1942). *The dictionary of philosophy.* New York: Philosophical Library.

Sattler, J. M. (2001). *Assessment of children: Cognitive applications* (4th ed.). La Mesa, CA: Sattler.

Salvia, J., Ysseldyke, J., & Bolt, S. (2013). *Assessment: In special and inclusive education* (12th ed.). Boston: Houghton-Mifflin.

Salzberg, C. L., Strain, P. S., & Baer, D. M. (1987). Meta-analysis for single-subject research: When does it clarify, when does it obscure. *Remedial and Special Education, 8*, 43–48.

Sanetti, L. M. H., Gritter, K. L., & Dobey, L. (2011). Treatment integrity of interventions with children in the school psychology literature from 1995 to 2008. *School Psychology Review, 40*, 72–84.

Sanetti, L. M. H., & Kratochwill, T. R. (2008). Treatment integrity in behavioral consultation: Measurement, promotion, and outcomes. *International Journal of Behavioral Consultation and Therapy, 4*, 95–114.

Sanetti, L. M. H., & Kratochwill, T. R. (2009). Toward developing a science of treatment integrity: Introduction to the special series. *School Psychology Review, 38*, 445–459.

Scruggs, T. E., Mastropieri, M. A., & Casto, G. (1987). The quantitative synthesis of single-subject research: Methodology and validation. *Remediate and Special Education, 8*, 24–33.

Shadish, W. R., & Rindskopf, D. M. (2007). Methods for evidence-based practice: Quantitative synthesis of single-subject designs. *New Directions for Evaluation, 113*, 95–109.

Shadish, W. R., Rindskopf, D. M. & Hedges, L. V. (2008). The state of the science in the meta-analysis of single-case experimental designs. *Evidence-Based Communication Assessment and Intervention, 3*, 188–196.

Shapiro, E. S., & Ager, C. L. (1992). Assessment of special education students in regular education programs: Linking assessment to instruction. *Elementary School Journal, 92*, 283–296.

Shepard, L. A. (2000). The role of assessment in a learning culture. *Educational Researcher, 29*(7), 4–14.

Shinn, M. R. (1989). Identifying and defining academic problems: CBM screening and eligibility procedures. In M. R. Shinn (Ed.), *Curriculum-based measurement: Assessing special children* (pp. 90–129). New York: Guilford Press.

Shinn, M. R. (2005). Identifying and validating academic problems in a problem-solving model. In R. Brown-Chidsey (Ed.), *Assessment for intervention* (pp. 219–246). New York: Guilford Press.

Sidman, M. (1960). *Tactics of scientific research: Evaluating experimental data in psychology.* New York: Basic Books.

Silberglitt, B., & Hintze, J. M. (2005). Formative assessment using CBM-R cut scores to track progress toward success on state mandated achievement tests: A comparison of methods. *Journal of Psychoeducational Assessment, 23*, 304–325.

Speece, D. L., & Case, L. P. (2001). Classification in context: An alternative approach to identifying early reading disability. *Journal of Educational Psychology, 93*, 735–749.

Speece, D. L., Case, L. P., & Molloy, D. E. (2003). Responsiveness to general education instruction as the first gate to learning disabilities identification. *Learning Disabilities Research and Practice, 18*, 147–156.

Stiggins, R. (2005). From formative assessment to assessment FOR learning: A path to success in standards-based schools. *Phi Delta Kappan, 87*, 324–328.

Sweet, A. P., & Snow, C. E. (2003). *Rethinking reading comprehension: Solving problems in the teaching of literacy.* New York: Guilford Press.

Tawney, J. W., & Gast, D. L. (1984). *Single subject research in special education.* Columbus, OH: Merrill.

Tilly, W. D. III, Batsche, G., Elliott, J., Graden, J. L., Grimes, J., Kovaleski, J. F., et al. (2005). *Response to intervention: Policy considerations and implementation.* Alexandria, VA: National Association of State Directors of Special Education.

Treptow, M. A., Burns, M. K., & McComas, J. J. (2007). Reading at the frustration, instructional, and independent levels: Effects on student time on task and comprehension. *School Psychology Review, 36*, 159–166.

VanAuken, T. L., Chafouleas, S. M., Bradley, T. A., & Martens, B. K. (2002). Using brief experimental analysis to select oral reading interventions: An investigation of treatment utility. *Journal of Behavioral Education, 11*, 165–181.

VanDerHeyden, A. M., & Burns, M. K. (2005). Using curriculum-based assessment and curriculum-based measurement to guide elementary mathematics instruction: Effect on individual and group accountability scores. *Assessment for Effective Intervention, 30*(3), 15–29.

VanDerHeyden, A. M., & Burns, M. K. (2009). Performance indicators in math: Implications for brief experimental analysis of academic performance. *Journal of Behavioral Education, 18*, 71–91.

VanDerHeyden, A. M., Witt, J. C, & Naquin, G. (2003). Development and validation of a process for screening referrals to special education. *School Psychology Review, 32,* 204–227.

Vollmer, T. R., Roane, H. S., Ringdahl, J. E., & Marcus, B. A. (1999). Evaluating treatment challenges with differential reinforcement of alternative behavior. *Journal of Applied Behavior Analysis, 32,* 9–23.

Wacker, D., Berg, W., Harding, J., & Cooper-Brown, L. (2004). Use of brief experimental analyses in outpatient clinic and home settings. *Journal of Behavioral Education, 13,* 213–226.

Wagner, R. K., Torgesen, J. K., & Rashotte, C. A. (1999). *Comprehensive test of phonological processing.* Austin, TX: Pro-Ed.

White, O. (1987). The quantitative synthesis of single-subject research: Method and validation: Comment. *Remedial and Special Education, 8,* 34–39.

William, D. (2006). Formative assessment: Getting the focus right. *Educational Assessment, 11,* 283–289.

Witt, J. C., Daly, E. M., & Noell, G. (2000). *Functional assessments: A step-by-step guide to solving academic and behavior problems.* Longmont, CO: Sopris West.

Yeo, S., Kim, D., Branum-Martin, L., Wayman, M. M., & Espin, C. A. (2011). Assessing the reliability of curriculum-based measurement: An application of latent growth modeling. *Journal of School Psychology. 50,* 275–292.

Ysseldyke, J., Burns, M. K., Scholin, S. E., & Parker, D. C. (2010). Instructionally valid assessment within response to intervention. *Teaching Exceptional Children, 42*(4), 54–61.

Zirkel, P. A., & Thomas, L. B. (2010). State laws and guidelines for implementing RTI. *Teaching Exceptional Children, 43*(1), 60–73.

Index

Page numbers followed by *f* indicate figure